RAINMAKING 101

How to Grow Your Client Base and Maximize Your Income

by
Patrick D. Kelly

authorHOUSE®

AuthorHouse™
1663 Liberty Drive, Suite 200
Bloomington, IN 47403
www.authorhouse.com
Phone: 1-800-839-8640

First published by AuthorHouse 1/22/2009

ISBN: 978-1-4389-5025-9 (sc)

Library of Congress Control Number: 2009900452

Printed in the United States of America
Bloomington, Indiana

This book is printed on acid-free paper.

Editing: Dan Page
Cover design: Natalie Belville
Book design: Dianne Schilling

To my family,
Donna, Joe and Jack

In memory of Edward F. Kelly

Limit of Liability

Acknowledgments

This book's journey from conception to completion was a long one, and a number of individuals helped along the way. I am grateful to Dan Page for his encouragement and meticulous editing, to Natalie Belville for her striking, spot-on cover design, and to Dianne Schilling for organizational advice, book design, and page layouts. In addition, special thanks go to Mark Blankenship, Forest Bowman, Dale Clowser, Deb Copeland, Kara Cunningham, David McKinley, Ed Mockler, Tom Wilkerson, and Kelly Young.

Contents

Introduction

Success usually comes to those who are too busy to be looking for it.
—Henry David Thoreau

What is rainmaking? That's a question I asked myself many years ago.

When I was in law school, my goal was to become a successful lawyer—a partner in a prestigious law firm. In school, I'd always achieved my goals by working and studying hard. After graduation, I thought all I had to do to become a partner was put my nose to the grindstone and work, work, work. However, a year or two after joining a firm, reality struck. Big law firms are *filled* with hard-working lawyers. Thousands of young, talented lawyers graduate from law school each year, and any one of them easily could replace me. Worse yet, everyone around me shared my goal of becoming a partner. It didn't take long to figure out that not everyone was going to make it. The search was on. I had to know: *What does it take to become a partner?*

The answer was not self-evident to me. I was not reared in a family of professionals. I had no idea what I needed to do. One day I asked one of the no-nonsense senior partners, "What is the key to becoming a partner?" Without hesitation, she replied, "You have to make the pie bigger. You have to become a rainmaker."

I walked away and sat in my office, dumbfounded. A rainmaker? My law school professors never mentioned anything about rainmaking. The only reference I had to the term "rainmaking" was from past history classes. I recalled stories of ancient people who claimed to have the ability to summon the gods to produce rain, but what could they have to do with law firms? Finally, I realized what the partner was trying to tell me. To become a partner, I needed to develop new clients and make money "rain down" on the law firm.

It actually made sense. Why would the partners in the firm share the wealth with me if I did the same thing everyone else did? I had to distinguish myself.

I understood the concept, but I didn't know how to begin making rain. I talked to my older friends who were insurance agents, stockbrokers, accountants, and junior executives, and I asked them what they knew about rainmaking. Surprisingly, most were familiar with the concept, but few knew how to make it happen. Soon I realized I was not alone. Millions of people embark on professional careers as CPAs, engineers, insurance agents, financial advisers, bankers, lawyers, and corporate managers only to discover that being technically proficient is just one element of being successful. Few receive any formal training in selling their services and themselves. For most, developing business is a sink-or-swim proposition.

Few things have changed over the years. Thousands of young professionals graduate each year and begin promising careers without any training in client development. What *has* changed is the need for rainmaking skills. The need for young entrepreneurial professionals who can make a great first impression, effectively communicate, and develop business relationships is greater than ever. Few people possess these basic skills. As technology has advanced, the methods by which we communicate have changed dramatically. Many young professionals are more accustomed to text messaging and instant messaging than having a direct conversation and, as a result, are uncomfortable in many social situations where direct communication and interaction are required to develop business relationships.

Although most communication in the workplace will take place in an indirect manner via technology, the occasions when strong, direct communication and interpersonal skills are necessary will become increasingly important. Most executives in the business world are more accustomed to, and demand, direct communication. The technological and communication gap that exists between young professionals and their superiors and clients is very pronounced. This gap represents an incredible opportunity. Young professionals who bridge this gap, focus on building relationships with people of all ages, and hone their direct communication skills—basic rainmaking skills—will surpass their peers and will dominate their fields.

Over the years, I have had the opportunity to meet and work with many successful people. I've watched, interviewed, and studied successful rainmakers to determine their secrets to success. I've learned that all of them were not born with "it"—the skills of a rainmaker. Successful people develop those skills, and they work at them. Obviously, each professional has his or her own style, but similarities do exist. No external factor makes them great at developing business; it is more of an internal factor, a drive from deep within, a self-discipline to stay focused. If I had to state a philosophy in one sentence, it would be: *Rainmakers simply do things that other people could do but don't want to do.* That statement, in a nutshell, is what this book is all about—identifying the traits, habits, and secrets that anyone can employ, but only a few choose to develop. Taking advantage of those personal traits, habits, and know-how requires discipline—the willingness to develop a routine that incorporates what you know and your drive to succeed. No one can do that for you.

This book is designed to provide a unique perspective—one that comes from someone who has struggled with the same challenges you face and has experienced both successes and failures. During your career, obvious and subtle opportunities will appear before you. This book aspires to help you make the most of each opportunity. Every idea and technique presented in this book might not be for everyone, but if you adopt a few and apply a little practice, a little imagination, and a little creativity, the only thing that won't be "little" will be the results.

Chapter I

The Power of Relationships

It's not what you know,
but who you know.
—unknown

Many self-help books make you plow through hundreds of pages before they reveal the guiding principle of their theory. Not here. In the first paragraph of this book, I am going to share with you the secret of rainmaking. Are you ready? The secret is: *It's all about relationships.*

That's it. It is so simple. Relationships are the core element of any business. Those who possess strong relationships have a huge competitive advantage over those who do not. The better you become at developing and maintaining relationships, the more successful you will become.

For some, the concept that "it's all about relationships" is incredibly frustrating. In fact, for some highly intelligent and skilled professionals, it absolutely drives them crazy. They see people of lesser talents and abilities achieving greater success. They wonder why clients aren't using them instead. They see average people promoted because of "connections" or "nepotism," and they don't understand. The answer is simple. It's all about relationships.

You don't have to like the fact that relationships play such a vital role in business, but you do need to recognize and accept it as fact. Whether it is right or not, you cannot change it because it involves basic human behavior. We all like to do business with people we know and trust or people with whom we have a connection. Instead of fighting this reality or ignoring it, I suggest you accept this fact and concentrate your energy on honing your relationship skills so you can effectively compete in your market.

What Is My Market?

Many young professionals actually have two markets in which they operate—an internal and an external market. Both are very important to your future and success.

If you work within an organization, your internal market—the people in your organization—cannot be ignored. Your superiors, colleagues, and subordinates will, to some extent, help or harm your progress. As such, it is very important to develop strong relationships at every level of your organization.

Your superiors are important because they will decide your future, and they also can be the people who help you the most. Superiors have the power to assign good and bad projects, mentor your professional development, control professional development opportunities, and regulate client contact. You want to be viewed as their "go-to person." This will open many opportunities. It also will force you to work harder and smarter. But that is part of the price of success.

Although superiors can decide your fate within the organization, colleagues and subordinates can seal your fate. What do I mean? The support staff and other professionals with whom you work can destroy your reputation quickly. How does that happen? Typically, it is subtle. If a superior asks a support staff member where you are, that staff member, instead of saying "at lunch," may reply "I don't know. He left for lunch an hour and a half ago." Another scenario might involve a superior checking on the status of a project, and a colleague responding, "I don't know if John is near completion. He is usually late on everything." These messages to superiors damage your credibility. I have told many young lawyers: "Your secretary or paralegal can be your best friend or your worst enemy. The choice is yours." Your colleagues can be the same. Unfortunately, you may never know whether someone is damaging your reputation until it is too late to address it. Most of the time, you will be fine if you treat people with dignity and respect and acknowledge the contributions they make. A few simple words of praise and encouragement, coupled with a "thank you," will do wonders.

Saying "I'm sorry" can work wonders as well. Researchers at Zogby, a leading public opinion pollster, found a direct correlation between apologies and income. They discovered that people who say "I'm sorry" make more money than people who rarely or never apologize. What's the connection? Zogby concluded that people who apologize have strong people skills. These people are more secure and have the ability to mend troubled relationships.

If further research were conducted, my guess would be that these high earners were successful, in part, because they built strong relationships within their organizations and had a dedicated team fully supporting their efforts.

Sharing the Limelight

To be truly successful within an organization, you must develop the habit of recognizing and acknowledging the contributions of others.

A Harvard professor who was hired to train a group of general agents for a big insurance company illustrated this point with an example. He asked the agents, "How many times have you stolen the limelight and taken the credit for other people's hard work and accomplishments? When your son scored a touchdown at the football game, have you ever stood up and yelled, 'That's my boy!'?" To drive the point home, the professor asked, "What do you say when your son fumbles the ball?" One wisecracker replied, "He has a lot of his mom in him."

While the wisecracker's quip may be humorous, it really illustrates how some people act within an organization. Everything that goes right is a result of their efforts alone. When things go wrong, it is someone else's fault.

Never focus all of the attention on yourself. Acknowledging the contributions of others is always the right thing to do. If you don't share the credit with others, you will never build internal relationships. Your colleagues won't trust you. They will always be suspicious of your every act and will find ways to sabotage you behind the scenes. If you look out only for yourself, you will always be alone and will lose the huge benefits that can be derived from teamwork. Success or failure is rarely the result of one person's efforts. Either one is the product of teamwork.

Regardless of whether you are developing internal relationships or external relationships, one thing holds true. *People don't care how much you know until they know how much you care.*

Be the most loyal co-worker and the most loyal employee to your organization. Strong relationships will develop, and success will follow.

Maintain Bridges

A natural extension of building relationships is maintaining relationships. Time and time again, I have observed young professionals destroy perfectly good relationships. This frequently occurs when they become frustrated with a superior or a colleague or when they leave one company to move to another. While it might feel good to let people know how you feel, it seldom helps your career in the long run. You need to show restraint. Never speak or act when you are frustrated or angry. If you can't get along with someone, try to find projects on which the objectionable person doesn't work. When you leave a company, leave on a positive note.

During the course of your career, you will be amazed by the number of times you will cross paths with former colleagues. Years from now, they may be in a position to award or deny you opportunities. The bottom line is: Never burn bridges.

The World of Clients

As you develop in your professional career, your "external market" will become increasingly important to achieving success. The external market is the world in which you offer your products and services. This is the market where competition is fierce and where relationships often take years to develop. Most of this book is focused on helping you develop relationships in the external market, but, as previously noted, many of the techniques mentioned in this book can help you build internal relationships as well.

How Do I Build Relationships?

No cookie-cutter approach exists for building relationships. Each relationship is unique to the two people involved. However, two basic principles apply to developing relationships—visibility and credibility.

First, you need to become aware *of* and become known *to* the person with whom you want to build the relationship. You need to become visible. This can be accomplished by becoming renowned in your field, attending business and social events, serving on boards, developing blogs, becoming involved in your community, speaking at seminars, publishing articles, or providing great service to existing firm clients.

Picking the proper forum for increasing your visibility is also important. If you offer a specialized service, go to the place where people who need that service congregate. Conrad Hilton, founder of one of the largest hotel organizations in the world, said, "If you want to launch big ships, you have to go where the water is deep." Find the place where the water is deepest for you. Industry associations are a great venue for marketing. Everyone has a similar interest. If you specialize in Medicare and Medicaid reimbusrement, attend association meetings of hospitals, nursing homes, and personal care homes. If you specialize in estate planning, go to places where wealthy people are likely to be—country clubs, upscale resorts, banks. Developing a relationship with a banker who can refer business to you makes sense. Think about your market and go to it. Don't wait for it to come to you.

Talk to your existing customers and find out what activities and meetings they attend. Are they members of a service organization or trade association? Are they members of a country club? Do they participate in any civic organizations? Ask them what publications they read. Submitting an article to that publication may be an option. Do they get information from the Internet? Creating a blog may be an option. Your goal is to find the forums in which you can become more visible to the people with whom you want to develop relationships.

Professionals often miss the mark. Lawyers, for example, often spend hours writing law review articles and legal treatises, and that is fine if you are trying to get referrals from other lawyers or want to impress the general counsel of a company. However, if your objective is to reach the CEO of a company, that person is unlikely to see the publication and, even if you send it to him, is unlikely to read it. Clients who are very busy and who are working in the trenches don't need that information. What they need is a short, precise, practical discussion on how to solve their problems or avoid problems. These folks are busy and don't have the time or the interest in an intellectual discussion. You could accomplish more by writing a series of shorter articles than a treatise on the law. That way, instead of the CEO receiving one thick paper with your name on it, he will receive several short articles that he actually may read. Additionally, your name will be in front of him more often, thereby heightening your visibility. You need to identify the relationship you want to develop and meet that person's need. Don't stay within your comfort zone. Reach out, and always stay focused on the other person's needs.

Credibility

The second key step in developing relationships is developing credibility. I cannot stress enough the importance of honesty, integrity, and character. These are the foundation of credibility. Reliability and trustworthiness are the building blocks.

As you read and study the techniques offered in this book, please do not view them as the end point in growing your client base. They are offered as a means to reach an end point and are intended to complement your other efforts as a professional. Strong marketing skills are not a replacement for core competency in your profession.

To be successful, you must be reliable and trustworthy. If you tell someone you will do something, you better do it and do it on time. Keeping promises is essential. For many people, credibility is the most difficult aspect of developing and maintaining relationships. For some, meeting people and developing an instant rapport is second nature. They seem to be born with that ability. But when it comes to delivering the goods, they fall apart. Following through on promises and commitments takes organization, hard work, and discipline. Many people won't put enough time and effort into maintaining a relationship. As a result, the relationship eventually deteriorates.

You have to know your limitations. Self-assessment is one of the most difficult things we have to do, but it is critical. Over-promising leads only to problems or failure. You probably know people who join every organization and volunteer for high-profile tasks to increase their visibility. Inevitably, most fail because of over-commitment or burnout. Others fail because they won't dedicate the time necessary to complete the task. In the end, all they achieve is a high-profile failure. The people they are trying to impress watch them fail and are left to clean up the mess. Why would anyone who witnessed that sort of result want to do business with a failure? As you begin your rainmaking, don't go to extremes. Don't spread yourself too thin, and don't quit before the project is completed. Instead, concentrate on doing a few things really well. You want to impress people and build credibility. In time, after performing a task very well, you can move on to a different position in the organization, or you can resign. Remember, always leave an organization or project on a high note with people impressed with your abilities. As the old axiom in the theater goes, "Leave them wanting more."

If you increase your visibility and develop credibility, you will be able to develop the relationships that will serve you well for years.

Generational Differences

Each successive generation in America views and develops business relationships in a slightly different manner. To be an effective rainmaker, you have to be aware of these differences and adjust for them when developing relationships. Cam Marston, an author and consultant on multigenerational relations and communications, studied for years the subtle differences in developing business relationships that exist between generations. According to Marston, Baby Boomers and Matures (Americans born before 1965) often want to develop a personal relationship with a person before "doing business" with that person. A Baby Boomer or Mature might say, "Show that you're interested in me. Ask me questions. Let's get to know one another, and then we'll enjoy doing business together." Baby Boomers and Matures place a high priority on knowing the people with whom they do business.

Visibility also is important. Baby Boomers and Matures view people who are leaders in their communities or highly regarded in their professions with greater credibility. Baby Boomers are part of the largest generation in history. From an early age, they were forced to be competitive to distinguish themselves from the crowd. As a result, they are extremely motivated by visible signs of success. Chairing the local hospital board or serving on the board of directors of a prestigious museum is important to them because it is a sign of achievement. As such, they value achievements obtained by others. To build relationships with members of this group, you need to recognize the activities or organizations that they value as important and become involved in them.

Members of the Generation X and the Millennial generation (Americans born between 1965 and 1980) have a different set of priorities. They value personal time and, as a result, efficiency is important. Generation Xers place a high value on people they perceive as being able to get the job done. Some refer to Generation Xers as the "prove-it-to-me" generation. They can be turned off by wining and dining and the "fluff" offered by some sales pitches. Generation Xers want to see substance up front. They are more likely to want to see a proposal that outlines your qualifications, plans for accomplishing the task, and the efficiencies that you will employ. They are more impressed by the person who will make their life easier than the person who will buy them drinks after work. In fact, they often want to go home after work to be with their families or pursue their personal interests. Marston describes their thought process as: "First, prove to me that you know what you are doing. I want a quick, thorough, and efficient transaction. After you've proved that to me, we might get to know one another." With the Generation X and Millennial generations, the relationship will develop after the credibility is firmly established.

Marston is not alone. Many generational experts agree that each generation in our work force today views work and the development of relationships differently. Highlighting these differences in generational attitudes is not to say that developing and maintaining a relationship is more important to one generation than the other. That is not the case. Relationships are important to all human beings. The point is that you have to develop relationships in different ways with different people. You have to be flexible. You need to think about the values and needs of the person with whom you want to develop the relationship. Every person who is a member of a specific generation, socioeconomic class, culture, or geographic locale does not think or act in the exact same manner, but similarities often exist. You simply need to recognize that one size does not fit all and be prepared to adapt.

Where to Start?

Begin your efforts to develop more business by examining your existing relationships. Have you sought business from your friends or family members? Sometimes people are simply waiting to be asked for their business. These people are your low-hanging fruit and are easy to pick. You should pick them first. If your friends and family won't do business with you, you have a problem. If this is the case, you must perform a serious self-assessment. Why won't the people who know you best do business with you? Do you lack credibility? If so, how can you change that perception? Whatever the problem, it likely will manifest itself when you establish other business relationships. If you fix it immediately, you will avoid a lot of problems in the future.

A second group that falls into the low-hanging fruit category consists of existing clients of your firm. This is an easy group to target because a relationship already exists. In large firms, clients occasionally get lost in the shuffle. Don't assume your firm is receiving all of a client's business. More opportunities may exist. Firms are notorious for "handing off" clients and not serving them well. Over the years, the attention and service these clients receive may dwindle. Look inside your firm and see whether you can find any of these clients.

Before approaching an existing client, talk to the person in the organization who is responsible for the relationship and discover his or her comfort level with your involvement in the relationship. Some people want total control and exclusive contact with clients, while others are open to involving others. Learn this before you step afoul.

If you receive the green light to become involved in the client relationship, the questions you need to ask yourself are, "Am I visible to the client?" and "Does the client view me as credible?" You may need to raise your profile with the client or demonstrate to him or her that you are competent. Make sure your credibility and your company's credibility are strong. If you have a contact inside the client's company, use this source for information. The more information you have, the better you will be at developing more work.

Keep in mind that a happy client is the best source of business that you have. It takes less time and effort to develop work from an existing client than prospecting for work from new leads. Additionally, happy clients are the best referral source you have. Prospective clients will listen to them because their recommendations are based on actual experience.

Referrals

As I just mentioned, client referrals are an excellent source of business. There is nothing wrong with asking existing clients for the names of other people who may need your product or service, but many professionals are reluctant to ask clients for referrals. Unfortunately, they lose a prime source of business and the rewards that go with it.

When a client does make a referral to you, treat that referral with great care. Never take on a project for a referral that you cannot accomplish. If you cannot deliver on your promises, you not only will lose the referral as a client, but you also will damage the relationship with your existing client. From your client's perspective, his or her reputation has just been damaged in the eyes of one individual. No one likes having his reputation impugned.

If your client is reluctant to offer a referral or can't think of anyone, be prepared with the name of someone you want to meet. A friend of mine who is a wealth planner always takes a few minutes before a meeting with a client to think about the various connections his client has to others. He reviews where the client lives, the organizations in which the client participates, family connections, and a variety of other associations his client might have. If a connection exists between the client and someone he would like to meet, he asks the client to make an introduction. The introduction might occur over the phone, via e-mail, at a social function, or, better yet, over a meal with the client and the new contact. For most people, making an introduction is not threatening. My friend claims that not one of his requests for an introduction has ever been denied. The secret, he claims, is to be sure that a strong connection exists between the client and the person you want to meet.

Remember, everybody likes to have their efforts acknowledged. When you do receive referrals or introductions from clients or other people, don't forget to thank them. Take the opportunity to build a stronger rapport and return the favor by referring business to them if they are reliable and trustworthy. Follow up with a call or an e-mail letting them know that you made the referral. Even if it does not pan out, your client or referral source will know that you are trying to help them. This is another great way to build relationships.

Go Deep

Business relationships often begin with one person in a company. You develop a great relationship with that person, and you stay so focused on that person's needs that you fail to look around. Don't forget about the others in the company. Too often people focus their entire attention on one person, develop a great relationship, and then forget about everyone else. Sometimes they make the others feel unimportant or excluded. When you invite your contact to play golf or attend some other activity, ask him to bring along a colleague. With companies downsizing and people changing jobs regularly, it is essential to establish deep and wide relationships in every business. The person you are ignoring or forgetting about today may be the person controlling the work tomorrow.

Always make an effort to expand your relationships throughout the organization. It will serve you well.

The Benefits Are Endless

Building relationships creates a huge competitive advantage.
In addition to providing you with referrals and lifelong clients,
strong relationships provide intangible benefits. If a client is comfortable with you and trusts you, he can provide you with valuable
information about his company and the people in it. You then
may be able to identify needs that the client did not know existed.
You may learn of future company plans and be able to anticipate
future needs. You may be able to identify the up-and-comers.

Perhaps most importantly, you may learn of problems that
exist within *your own* organization. People often don't like to
convey bad news. It is easier for them to move their business to
another firm than engage in confrontation. If you can discover
problems that your client is experiencing with your organization,
you can correct them before they get out of control and a valued
customer is lost. It is amazing the little things that upset people
and how easy it is to solve those problems. Identifying and fixing
problems can greatly enhance your credibility. Gaining information
from an insider who trusts you and who is comfortable discussing
things with you is essential to providing top-quality service.

Discipline

Building relationships takes self-discipline. The principles
you are learning from this book require constant refinement and
implementation. You can't work at building relationships for a
couple of weeks and then take a month off. You have to focus on
it and work at it every day, even when you don't feel like it.

A retired insurance agent who was fantastic at building relationships and was wildly successful summed up the relationship
process perfectly: "Relationships are like baking. You have to put
something in before you take anything out."

The pages that follow will provide you with various ingredi-
ents that you can put into building strong relationships. As your
relationships grow, be prepared. New business and opportunities
will rain down on you.

Chapter II

First Impressions

Men in general judge more from appearances than from reality.
All men have eyes, few have the gift of penetration.
—Machiavelli

The adage is true. First impressions *are* lasting impressions. The survival instincts of humans cause us to make snap decisions about people. Immediately upon seeing someone, we instinctively determine whether a person is a threat to us. Once we have determined that we are safe, we begin to make other quick judgments. We form numerous opinions about people within seconds of meeting them. In fact, studies indicate that first impressions are made within seven seconds of meeting someone, and more than half of the first impression is based on nonverbal cues, such as an individual's behavior and appearance.

Think about your own personal experiences. How many times have you formed an instant opinion about someone based on how he was dressed or how he carried himself? Have you ever said to yourself, "This lady is really sharp!" or "That guy looks like a jerk!" based only on a few seconds' observation of someone you have never seen before? We all do it; it is simply human nature.

From a rainmaking perspective, it is important to give a good first impression because it opens the door to developing a relationship with a person. When we talk about first impressions, we often are talking about perception versus reality. And, sad to say, reality is not as important as perception, at least initially. Remember, a person's perception *is* his or her reality. If you cannot project an image that is perceived well, people often won't give you the chance to prove otherwise. If someone gets the impression you are sloppy, lazy, boring, or offensive, then you *are* sloppy, lazy, boring, and offensive until you have an opportunity to prove otherwise. Once a person forms a negative impression of you, then you must work harder to show who you really are. So creating the *perception* that you are decent, competent, and honest—the type of person with whom others may want to do business some day—is very important. Creating a perception of success also is important because people are attracted to successful individuals.

So let's talk about that first impression.

Confidence Is Quintessential

Self-confidence is one of the most important personal messages you convey to a new acquaintance. People want to do business with and turn their problems over to someone who is self-assured. Amazingly, we all possess some ability to sense fear and intimidation. When we do, we are less likely to have trust and confidence in the individual projecting those qualities. Therefore, it is essential for you to convey an air of self-assurance immediately. Conveying confidence alleviates people's concerns and anxieties and makes them more willing to give you business.

Exhibiting self-confidence does not mean you have to be loud or overbearing. You don't have to possess a huge ego. In fact, those characteristics can turn people off. Self-confidence manifests itself in being comfortable with who you are as a person.

No formula exists for developing confidence. It is a uniquely individual characteristic. Many confident and successful people will attest that a positive attitude is essential to success. Sensing that you *can* succeed actually helps you succeed. For some, being comfortable in the environment in which they work or meet people makes them more confident. When they want to exhibit a greater sense of personal confidence, some people dress up or do something extra that makes them feel special. Find the little things that make you feel more confident and use them regularly. As our self-confidence improves, we more effectively radiate that confidence to others.

When I was in high school, I often wondered why some boys always had dates and others didn't. Years later, I can see one quality that separated the two groups of boys. One group was very self-confident, and the other group was not. The boys who were confident and were not afraid to talk to girls always got the dates. Their counterparts who were shy and awkward sat at home on Saturday night. Have you ever asked yourself, "How did that guy get a date with that nice girl?" The answer probably is simple. He asked her. Moreover, he asked her because he was not afraid of being rejected. The fear of failure stops many people in their tracks and affects their ability to make rain.

In business, you have to have the confidence to ask. Even though you may not feel confident, you can always project confidence through your attitude and the nonverbal cues you convey to others. Walking tall, speaking in an appropriate tone, maintaining strong eye contact, extending a firm hand shake, and initiating contact all are conscious behaviors you can choose to project a sense of confidence even when you feel less than sure of yourself.

Shaking Hands

A handshake is the most personal contact you will have with a stranger, and through it you will convey an extremely important nonverbal message. Often I have heard people say, "You can tell a lot about a man by the way he shakes your hand." The same is true of a woman. Now you are probably saying to yourself, "I already know how to shake hands. This is ridiculous."

You would be amazed at the number of professional people who convey poor impressions with their handshakes. Would you have confidence in someone whose hand feels like a jellyfish when you shake it, or would you want to be a partner on a project with someone who crushes your hand like an 800-pound gorilla trying to squeeze a banana out of its peel? Of course not. The jellyfish appears weak, and the gorilla appears overbearing.

The person with the weak handshake may, in fact, be a very strong person, while the "gorilla" may be a pushover. But the handshake conveys an impression.

In addition to the strength of your grip, keep in mind the length of your handshake. Do you grab a person's hand, shake it, and then toss it away? If so, you may be conveying several non-verbal messages. You may be telling the person that he or she is not worth your time, or you may be conveying shyness or a lack of confidence.

Every society has its cultural norms—rules that govern what is acceptable or unacceptable. Among the subtlest of these rules are those focused on touch. Even within the same society, some folks are "touchy-feely" while others are more distant. So how do you deal with a stranger whose attitudes on touch and intimacy are unknown to you? The answer: very carefully.

Grasp the stranger's hand firmly, but not too firmly, pump it once or twice, and let go. If you barely make contact, you may convey the message that you are uninterested. But if you hold on too long you can give the opposite impression—that "something is going on here." Don't laugh. Mrs. Norman Vincent Peale once said of her husband of more than 60 years: "I knew Norman was interested in me the first time I shook hands with him after a church service because he held my hand just an instant too long!"

We all have shaken hands with someone who wouldn't let go. At some indefinable point you stopped *shaking* hands and started *holding* hands. And chances are you felt uncomfortable. The last thing you want to do if you are trying to create a good first impression is cause the person you are meeting to feel uncomfortable. Touching—even in the ritualized handshake—is charged with emotion.

What message does your handshake send? Ask your friends and close business associates. If they say it shows confidence, fine. If they say it is weak, work on strengthening it. If they consistently say that it doesn't leave them with any impression, then think about the impression you want to send and how a person making that impression would shake hands. Now, practice duplicating that image.

The handshake is a wonderful opportunity to tell a stranger something positive about you. Make the most of this opportunity. Create the perception that you want others to experience and start now.

As we'll discuss later, eye contact is also an important component in the first impression. As such, when shaking hands, you must be sure to make eye contact. Failure to do so shows a lack of true interest regardless of your handshake.

Appearance

Many books and articles have been written about what to wear and what not to wear. I won't even try to duplicate them. Most of the time, common sense should prevail. Generally, you just need to know two things: first, who you will be around, and, second, the environment in which you will be.

Let's start with work. Who will you be around? Most likely, you will be around other professionals. Professionals tend to dress up. Second, what environment will you be in? You most likely will be in a climate-controlled office environment. People in this type of office environment tend to dress up. So far, the answer is easy: You should dress up at work. However, dressing up has many different meanings.

In a traditional old law firm, dressing up may mean a suit. In a small insurance agency, it may mean slacks and a collared shirt. The key is to look around you. What are the established people in the company wearing? More importantly, what are the partners or supervisors wearing? I am a firm believer that you don't dress for the job that you have. You dress for the job that you *want* to have. It is easier for members of management to envision you in a higher position if you already look like you belong there.

Keep in mind that you can't follow the lead of just any person in the office because every office has a rebel. This is the person who always pushes the fashion envelope. He or she may be the most fun and probably will embrace you the fastest. But he or she probably drives the older members of management crazy—the same people who set salaries and award promotions. My best advice is to follow the lead of many others and then develop your own personal style along the way.

What about the after-work event? You are invited to a cookout at a partner's home, and you are told that dress is casual. A red flag should go up in your brain. Beware: The term "casual" has many different meanings as well. You may be thinking fraternity or sorority party casual or beer-keg casual. Shorts and flip-flops may come to mind.

If the party is at the 60-year-old partner's house, I doubt that fits his definition of casual. For members of the Mature generation and early Baby Boomers, casual often means a sports coat or a dress. So what do you do? Ask two or three people who have been at the firm for at least a few years what people typically wear to these events. Never ask, "What can I wear?" Trying to be nice, the person might say shorts and flip-flops are all right. But if you ask what others typically wear, or what a colleague plans to wear, the answer might be khaki slacks, a collared shirt, and a blazer.

Remember, as a young professional, you don't want to look like a kid. You want to look like a responsible person who can handle important tasks. Also, don't forget that you want to impress spouses as well. Often, I hear professionals say, "I'm not a good judge of character, but my husband is and he thought. . . ." Keep in mind that many people are evaluating you in the early years of your professional career.

If you are invited to a social event, keep the same principles in mind. Think about the people who will attend and the environment. I failed to follow my own advice one time and, boy, did I feel stupid. My wife and I received an invitation to a reception celebrating a wedding that took place about a month earlier. The invitation was bright and colorful and had a tropical flair. The husband and wife hosting the event were both older, well-established professionals in the community, and the event was at 6 o'clock in the evening at the nicest country club in town. That darn invitation threw me. I wore an open-collared, bright orange shirt with a blazer, trying to keep with what I thought would be a tropical theme. Well, you guessed it: All the men were dressed in business suits and ties, and the women wore cocktail dresses. I believe that I was the only male without a tie, and I am certain that I was the only male in a bright orange shirt. Did I ever stick out—like a sore (orange) thumb!

If I had thought about the people who would be attending the reception—professionals who were in their 50s and 60s—and where the reception was held—a very nice country club—the clothing choice would have been obvious. Even the time—the cocktail hour—should have been a clue. That evening, I felt like a little kid, and I hid in the back of the room. I knew better.

Personally, I always feel better when I am a bit overdressed rather than underdressed. It is easier to remove a tie or take off a blazer than to put one on. For young professionals, I think it is important to always look sharp and not overly fashion-trendy.

I can't stress enough the importance of thinking about the impression that you may be creating by your personal appearance.

Watch the Ends

A friend of mine who is a state senator and a successful insurance salesman maintains that you have to "watch the ends" when dealing with older people. What are the ends? Your hair and your shoes. Older people were taught the importance of keeping their hair coiffed and their shoes shined. And when they do business with people, they look for those signs. If you plan to do business with older Americans, keep this in mind. It will help you build credibility.

Personal Space

When you talk to someone, think about the distance you keep from that person. Surrounding each one of us is an invisible space that is "our" space and into which we let only those with whom we feel very comfortable. The actual size of the space varies from society to society and, within any particular society, it will vary depending on any number of factors. In the eastern United States, for example, this space is generally conceded to be about 18 inches. That is to say, when someone approaches you, you tend to become uncomfortable when that person gets closer than 18 inches from your body. Usually you will not realize *why* you are uncomfortable. You generally will know only that this person makes you uncomfortable. The environment where you live or the cultural norms with which you are familiar greatly dictate personal space. For example, people from large cities tend to need less personal space because they are accustomed to being crowded. People who live in wide open spaces tend to need greater personal space. In the western states and Alaska, where population is less dense and space is wide open, the need for personal space tends to be greater.

One westerner explained the phenomenon this way: "I was raised on a ranch in Wyoming, and our closest neighbor was 75 miles away. I just don't feel comfortable being physically close to other people!"

Cultural norms also play a role in personal space. A friend described a woman from Naples, Italy, who moved into his neighborhood. She was a lovely woman, but she made all of the neighbors feel very uncomfortable. She had the most irritating way of getting right up in people's faces when she talked to them. If they backed away, she came forward. As a result, the neighbors tended to feel uncomfortable in her presence. But this woman grew up in southern Italian culture where it was common (and certainly not rude) to be physically very close when talking to another person. When they realized that, my friend and his wife began to feel more comfortable in her presence.

Why is personal space important to rainmaking? Because if you recognize and respect a person's need for personal space, you can make that person feel more comfortable. If he or she is comfortable, you gain a huge advantage in developing a relationship and in doing business with that person.

Eye Contact

Your eyes are one of the most important communication devices you possess. If used effectively, your eyes can convey power, interest, and confidence. You will notice that powerful businessmen and women and politicians use eye contact to captivate and control people. Many parents control their children's behavior with a quick glance or glare, and advertisers prompt us to buy products we don't need through the captivating eyes of models.

All charismatic and powerful Americans I have met have one common habit. They maintain strong eye contact. This habit conveys a variety of non-verbal messages—strength, interest, warmth, appreciation. If you don't feel comfortable using strong eye contact, practice. It can be developed over time.

Poor eye contact also sends a message. When people look away during a conversation or look away immediately after they meet someone, they convey a negative message. They may appear to be embarrassed, unworthy, submissive, untrustworthy, or simply uninterested. Looking away is usually a reflex reaction that can be corrected if you set your mind to it.

Practice looking people squarely in their eyes when you talk to them. Do this with everyone you meet, whether you already know them or not, until it becomes second nature. If you are unaccustomed to looking directly into people's eyes, it will be difficult at first. In fact, you may feel very uncomfortable. To overcome this feeling, simply pretend you are having a staring contest. Remember staring at your childhood friend to see who would blink first? Try a little of that. Continue making eye contact even after you begin to feel uncomfortable. In time, you'll be able to look a new contact in the eye and convey confidence.

Another trick is to look at the person's forehead or between his eyes. You will appear to be looking at that person and will break the nervous reflex of looking away.

Cultural norms also come into play when eye contact is used. Certain cultures, such as Native American, Mennonite, and Japanese, view strong eye contact as inappropriate in certain circumstances. In fact, strong eye contact can be viewed as aggressive or downright rude. Although you have to know who you are dealing with, our society overall requires strong eye contact from its successful people. You need to learn to do it.

Quality Time and Attention

Pay close attention to people when they talk to you. Noted psychologist Dr. Joyce Brothers believes "listening, not imitation, may be the sincerest form of flattery." Listen not only with your ears but also with your eyes and body. Poor listeners tend to look around a room and fidget. Such behavior conveys three strong messages to the speaker: (1) He is uninteresting; (2) the topic is boring; and (3) you can't wait to get away. Although those feelings may be true, you don't want to convey that message to a potential client, business associate, or referral source. A rainmaker's goal is to end every conversation with the speaker believing that he is the most interesting person on this earth. When you make a person feel good about himself, you will be remembered.

E. Gordon Gee, who served as president of several prestigious universities, including Brown and Vanderbilt, raised the simple act of paying attention to an art form. He would walk through a crowd, stopping for a few minutes to talk to each person. By the time the evening was over, everyone in the room believed Dr. Gee was his or her personal friend. All that this savvy gentleman did was maximize the time he spent with each person. He would look each person in the eye, listen attentively, and give the person his undivided attention, even if he spent only 30 seconds with each of them. He made everyone feel important. His career soared in large part because of his personal skills and ability to build relationships. Dr. Gee made the most of his skill of listening. The same can happen for you.

Think Before You Act

To make a good first impression, you need to think about the people you will encounter and properly prepare to meet them.

One of the greatest business *faux pas* I have ever heard of occurred when a new associate in a law firm walked into a meeting with Coca-Cola executives carrying a can of Pepsi. The situation became worse when one of the executives asked her why she didn't drink Coke. She replied, "I can't stand the taste of that stuff." Needless to say, that first impression did not go well.

So what have we learned in this chapter? Experience and observation tell us that details matter as we develop relationships with others. Recognizing and implementing customary social practices make a difference. Personal conduct matters. The way we greet people, speak to people, and generally present ourselves can determine whether we are given the opportunity to develop lasting relationships. These details can foster trust that leads to both personal and business relationships.

The stranger you meet today by chance could become your best client tomorrow if you make a good, strong first impression.

Chapter III

Remembering Names

*Remember that a man's name is,
to him, the sweetest and most
important sound in any language.*
—Dale Carnegie

For many of us, remembering names is difficult, but make no mistake: It is extremely important in building relationships. People like to hear their own names. It has been said that the sweetest sound in the world is hearing one's own name. If that is true, and I believe it is, then we must place great importance on learning names. When you remember a person's name, you make that person feel important, and you begin to establish a personal rapport. One of my friends claims he cannot remember names, yet he can memorize the batting statistics of dozens of Major League baseball players. The fact is he *can* remember names. He simply doesn't place any importance on doing so. You need to make a conscious decision to remember names and place a high priority on it. If you apply yourself and use a few helpful tools, you can do it.

Word Association

When you meet a new person, try to associate the person's name with something you like, such as a place, object, actor, phrase, color, or animal. "Ralph Wilson looks like Tom Hanks." "Mike-Maryland." "Jean-Jaguar."

Turning names into pictures also may help. For a person named Barney, you might think of a barn. For Katrina, visualize a cat.

Try different associations until you find something that works for you.

Repetition

Repetition is a very effective way to learn any type of information. If you think about the poems, prayers, and stories that you can recite from memory, chances are you remember them because you said them or heard them over and over again. Why do more people know the words to the Pledge of Allegiance than the "Star Spangled Banner"? Because they said the Pledge of Allegiance every day at school. Repetition is a very strong tool that works in our conscience and our subconscious. You can use this important tool to help you remember names.

Repeat Names Aloud

When you are introduced to a new person, listen carefully for her name. Most people don't catch the person's name because they are too busy thinking about the next thing they want to say, and they aren't listening. After a person says his name, repeat it aloud while you shake hands. For example, someone introduces you to Jim Brown. When you extend your hand, say, "Jim Brown, it is nice to meet you." This exercise allows you to repeat the new person's name and assures that you have learned the name correctly. If you didn't learn the name correctly, Jim likely will correct you in a polite manner. This habit is extremely effective because of its simplicity.

Repeat, Repeat, Repeat

When you meet someone new, repeat his name three times. If you are uncomfortable doing that aloud, say it to yourself three times. This experience will help you remember his name.

How do you say a person's name aloud three times without looking ridiculous? The first time is when you shake the person's hand and say, "Jim Brown, it is nice to meet you." After that, during the course of your conversation with Mr. Brown, work his name into the conversation. The easiest way to do that is by saying the person's name before a question. "Jim, how do you think the Steelers will do this year?"

Instead of asking, "Where are you from?" ask "Jim, where are you from?" You can incorporate the person's last name by saying something like, "Is the Brown family originally from Pittsburgh?" This will keep the conversation at a more personal level. By sporadically saying your new acquaintance's name, you will reinforce it in your mind. Moreover, the sense of familiarity will hasten the development of a relationship.

If another person is present, immediately introduce your new acquaintance to that person. "Gloria, do you know Jim Brown?" By saying his name, you again reinforce your memory.

Learn the Name Correctly

Remembering someone's name incorrectly is very dangerous because it may be difficult to change what you have learned. Don't hesitate to ask someone to repeat his or her name when you are introduced. Often people are introduced or introduce themselves hurriedly, and you can't understand the name you hear. It is important to ask them to repeat their name so you can learn it and learn it correctly.

Some names are complicated. Ask for help with complicated names and make a sincere effort to pronounce the name correctly. Never respond by saying, "That is a mouthful," or some other disrespectful statement. You may feel embarrassed about asking, but remember, it is not about your comfort level. The goal is to make your new acquaintance feel respected.

Seeing Is Remembering

If you are a person who learns by seeing things rather than hearing things, look at the person's nametag. Seeing the name written may reinforce it in your memory.

Also, ask your new acquaintance for her business card. For visual learners, seeing the person's name on the card may help you remember it. Moreover, you can refer to the card later to reinforce your memory. Place the business cards you collect in a drawer or envelope with other names and cards you have collected and review them on a regular basis. That will help you memorize through repetition. Better yet, purchase client relationship-management software to keep track of your contacts or create a database of your own that you can access easily.

I Can't Remember His Name!

Have you ever been in the situation where you see someone you know but you just can't remember his name? It happens to me all the time. I will remember the face and some detail about the person, but I just can't think of his name or I am not sure what his name is. If this happens to you, try the following tips:

Introduction plan. If you attend an event with a spouse or friend, develop a plan to help each other. If one of you does not immediately say the name of a person, the other person's job is to extend his hand and introduce himself. The mystery person likely will introduce himself and you can hear the name.

Third-party pass. If a person enters a conversation and you can't remember his name, introduce this mystery person to a person whose name you do know. "Have you ever met Bill Perkins?" The mystery person will likely complete the introduction himself.

Ask for a phone number. When you encounter a person you have not seen in a long time and cannot remember his or her name, hand that person a blank piece of paper and ask him to write his telephone number or e-mail address on it. Inevitably, he will not only write the requested information, but he will also write his name next to it. When he hands it back to you, just take a quick peek, and you will learn his name! It is amazing how this little trick works, especially with phone numbers.

Business Meetings

When you go to a business meeting and suddenly find yourself at a table with several people you don't know, draw a diagram of the table with a star marking the place where you are sitting. As people introduce themselves around the table, write their names on the diagram at the places they are sitting. You may only have time to write first names, and that is all right. You can fill in last names later. If you miss a name, leave a blank space and listen for someone else to say the name during the meeting. When you hear the name, write it in the empty spot on the diagram. If you don't have paper, offer each person a business card and politely ask for their business card. When the people around the table introduce themselves, arrange the business cards in a pattern based upon where the people are seated at the table.

Time Is of the Essence

Remembering people's names is extremely important in developing relationships. It is critically important to concentrate on learning a person's name as soon as you meet her. Odds are you will not learn a person's name if you do not learn it within the first 30 seconds of meeting her. Remembering names is a skill and, like any skill, it takes time and practice to develop.

Practice Time

Are you interested in practicing any of these techniques? Turn on the TV and watch a movie. Try to remember the names of all of the characters who appear in the movie. It can be quite challenging, and it is great practice.

Chapter IV

Making Yourself Memorable

When you do the common things in life in an uncommon way,
you will command the attention of the world.
—George Washington Carver

Part of becoming a good rainmaker is getting people to remember *your* name. This feat is equally important to your remembering the names of the people you meet. How else are people
going to know who to call when they need your services?

During the course of our professional lives, we meet hundreds
if not thousands of people, many of whom we will remember only
for a few minutes after meeting them. How, then, can we make
ourselves more memorable to others? That is a difficult task. Obviously, making a good first impression is important because this
makes people want to remember us, but we must do more to
reinforce our presence in the minds of others.

Introductions: Slow and Clear

Because remembering names is difficult for most people, you need to help them. One simple way to help other people remember your name is to introduce yourself slowly and clearly. Enunciate your first name clearly and loudly, and then pause for a second before you say your last name. Initially this will feel awkward and sound unnatural, but it allows the listener time to hear and learn your full name.

Another technique in assisting people to learn your name is to give your last name first and then your whole name. You might call this the Bond technique: "Bond, James Bond." This method gives the listener two opportunities to hear your last name.

Too often people blurt their name so quickly that it is practically unintelligible. If the listener can't understand your name, there is no point in saying it. Be proud of your name and say it with distinction. Mumble it, and not only will no one hear and remember it, but you will suggest that it is not important or that you are not proud of it. This certainly is not the message you want to convey.

Finally, at the end of the conversation, if it is appropriate, give the listener your business card. This practice gives him or her a second opportunity to learn your name, and, once tucked away, the card will reappear at a later date to reinforce your name.

Reintroduce Yourself

Another technique for helping new acquaintances remember your name is to reintroduce yourself when you see them: "Hi, Bill. Henry Brown. It's nice to see you again." This habit reinforces your name with the listener and avoids embarrassing him if he can't remember your name. Too often, our egos get in the way, and we want to see whether others remember us. This is unproductive. Your goal is not to test the other person's ability to remember names or to soothe your own ego. Rather, your objective is to drill your name into the listener's memory. The other person likely will appreciate the effort.

One of the worst things you can do is walk up to someone you barely know or haven't seen in years and say: "Hi, Joe. Do you remember me?" You immediately place the person in an uncomfortable and potentially embarrassing position. Why place the person in an awkward position? Try saying something like, "Hi, Joe. I'm Henry Brown. Do you remember me from high school?" Your friend will enjoy the conversation much more.

Personal Notes

More than one way exists to make favorable impressions. While personal contact is an excellent way to communicate and get to know new people and new business prospects, it is not the only way. For example, cards and letters are an old-fashioned means of communication, but they certainly convey information and sentiment in a way that is almost certain to stand out.

For a special touch, send a personal note to a friend or new acquaintance. Personal, handwritten notes always are appropriate and are a great way to stand out in an e-mail/text message-driven society. A short, simple, handwritten note to someone you just met will accomplish a number of rainmaking goals. First, the note will increase your visibility, and, second, it will make the person feel special because you have taken the time to write him. Remember, you always want to leave people with the feeling that you think they are special and interesting. Hopefully, you've already done that in your brief conversation at the event. A follow-up note will reinforce your sincerity. Third, a handwritten note is a rarity these days. You will stand out from the crowd in a very positive way. Finally, the note will reinforce *your* name. Remember: Your goal is not only to learn the names of other people but also to get others to remember your name.

Early in my career, I had the honor to serve as general counsel to the governor of West Virginia. Governor Cecil H. Underwood had the distinction of serving as the youngest governor in the state's history and the oldest governor. His political career spanned more than six decades. He was unusually shy for a politician but was good at building and maintaining relationships. Almost daily, during breaks and between meetings, he would write handwritten notes to people on a variety of subjects. Many would fall into the category of thank-you notes. In fact, I recall one special thank-you note. Governor Underwood received a beautiful thank-you note from a constituent. He was touched and immediately grabbed his pen and stack of cards and envelopes and wrote a thank-you note to the constituent for the thank-you note he received. The staff howled. The governor simply said, "She put a lot of time and effort into that note, and I wanted her to know that it made my day."

Two important observations can be gleaned from this episode. First, the governor knew the importance of writing notes to build and maintain relationships. Second, a man who wrote notes all of the time was moved by receiving one himself. Personal notes are very powerful. People loved receiving notes from the governor. They couldn't imagine that he took the time out of his busy schedule to write them. I believe his personal notes were especially effective because such correspondence is no longer commonplace in society. They truly were special. Moreover, the governor gave each recipient a piece of his time, and that made them feel special.

I have tried to incorporate this practice in my life, and I encourage you to do the same. Buy a box of printed note cards with your name on them, and send friends and business acquaintances notes to acknowledge successes, celebrate family, and keep in touch. Having printed cards on hand will allow you to act spontaneously.

Here are four examples of basic notes:

Follow-up to a meeting

Dear Jim,

It was a pleasure meeting you at the Chamber of Commerce Dinner last week. Best wishes to you and your wife on the future addition to your family.

Sincerely,
John Smith

Follow-up with information

Dear Susan,

After our conversation about gardening last week at the Smith wedding, I
came across the enclosed article on
fall gardening that I thought might
be of interest to you.

Yours truly,
Amy Jones

Awards

Dear Susan:

Congratulations on your receipt of
the Goodwill Industries award. I am
pleased that Goodwill recognized your
hard work, and I want you to know
that I appreciate your contribution
to the community as well.

Most sincerely,
Warren Jones

Weddings*

Dear John:

Congratulations on your recent nup-
tials. Mary and I wish you and your
bride great happiness.

Please extend our best wishes to
Betty.

Sincerely,
Elizabeth Parsons

* The groom is always congratulated, and best wishes are extended to the bride.

Your note does not have to be elaborate, but it should incorporate information that will help the recipient recall you. At a minimum, the note should contain the name of the event where you met the person, a reference to your conversation, and your first and last name.

Many other opportunities exist for writing notes to friends and new acquaintances: promotions, career changes, public service, awards, births, and deaths, to name a few. People absolutely love receiving and reading them. You should discipline yourself to write notes. Prepare a file where you can place newspaper clippings and memos to yourself about the notes you should write. Then set aside one hour each week to write them.

I often dictate a rough draft of a note and ask my secretary to type it and obtain the individual's address. After I get it back, I either place it in my file or make any minor modifications as needed. Later, I handwrite the note on my stationery. This exercise allows me to write the note while I am thinking about it and review it later when I have time to hand write it. It also ensures accurate spelling via the spelling check on the computer.

Keep the notes personal and don't solicit business in them. In some instances, it may be appropriate to send the note on a note card that discreetly displays the name of your business. In other instances, that may be inappropriate. When in doubt, use personal stationery. It is always the safest.

The important thing to remember is that, when writing notes, you are building personal relationships, not seeking business. Business may or may not flow from any one relationship you build. But the laws of nature suggest one inevitability: The greater the number of personal relationships you have, the more business you will develop.

The Loss of a Loved One

I also keep a box of sympathy cards in my desk drawer. The sense of loss that a person experiences at the death of a loved one is truly enormous. Because of their age, many young professionals have not experienced such a significant loss, so they do not fully understand the tremendous effect a sympathy card can have. People appreciate others remembering them at such times.

Take the time to send a card. If you wait to purchase a card, you often will forget, so keep a box of sympathy cards handy and use them.

Record Important Dates

When a customer or referral source tells you about an upcoming date that is important to him, record it and follow up with a note or call. Here's an example: Your client tells you that he is moving his office in two months. Record the anticipated move date, then check to see whether the move actually occurred. If it did, acknowledge the event in some fashion. Your client will be impressed that you took such a keen interest. Most computer systems have excellent calendars and reminder features that are too simple not to use.

Patronize Your Clients

Whenever possible, spend your money where you make your money. If you are an accountant for a clothing store, make sure you purchase some of your clothes from that store. Your client will notice and appreciate your patronage, and, best of all, you may learn a little more about your client's business. If you expect loyalty from your clients, you must demonstrate your loyalty to them. Supporting their businesses is one way to do it. You will truly make yourself memorable.

Be Sincere

Someone hustles your clients every day. Your clients don't need more of the same. They need someone they can trust and rely on. Be sincere in everything you do. I once asked a very flamboyant public relations man why he was so successful. His reply was simple: "I'm a big bullshitter, but I am very sincere." He recognized that the core of his success was not his gift of gab. It was a love for what he did and the people for whom he did it. You must be sincere in everything you do.

Be Creative

Many people think being creative is difficult and swear they don't have a creative bone in their body. Regardless, you can find many ways to make yourself memorable. A friend with the name Slagel tells people that her name rhymes with "bagel."

On St. Patrick's Day, an Irish friend delivers green cakes to friends and clients.

My friend Mark, who is a big college football fan, wanted to strike up a relationship with the university's new coach. Every time he saw the coach, he would introduce himself and jokingly tell the coach his problem would be solved if he ran the wishbone offense. Now the coach knows his name and refers to him as "Wishbone."

A fellow I met in college, John, knew all the pretty girls on campus. Between classes, he always was talking to one. One day, I asked him how he got to know all of them. He grinned and said, "OK, I'll tell you my secret. I find out their names, and whenever I pass by them, I say hello and their first name—'Hello, Kim.' Over time, I strike up a little conversation like, 'How was your weekend' and 'Are you going to the game on Saturday.' Just a little small talk. After a while, they become curious and ask around and try to find out my name, and then we start talking more and more." As ridiculous as it sounds, it actually works.

I first tried this tactic on an older businessman I wanted to meet. Every few days, I saw him on the elevator. I started saying, "Good morning, Mr. Plarno." At first, he courteously said, "Good morning." After a while, I started commenting on the weather, sports, civic events—whatever I could think of. Several weeks after I began this, I stepped into the elevator and said, "Good morning, Mr. Plarno." He smiled and said, "Good morning, Pat." I was shocked that he had learned my name. It worked. He found out my name, and we were friends for years.

With just a little effort or creativity on your part, you have the ability to make others remember you. And being remembered is essential to rainmaking.

Chapter V

Cocktail Chatter

Half this game is ninety percent mental.
—Yogi Berra

Effective rainmakers communicate well with others. However, for many, talking to strangers and engaging in small talk is difficult and stressful. This anxiety is very natural, but you can employ various strategies to make it easier. Talking to people is an important component in building strong relationships. This chapter provides you with a little perspective on how some people think and react, along with ideas to keep a conversation alive.

The Sign

Every person in the world wears an invisible sign that says, "Make me feel important!" If you think about this sign every time you meet a new person, you will know exactly what to do. You will treat the person with respect, communicate a positive message, give the person your undivided attention, and talk about things that make that person feel good.

Let People Talk About Themselves

When you first meet someone, it often is difficult to strike up a conversation because you don't know the person's interests, attitudes, or general demeanor. There is, however, one subject everyone knows about—*themselves*. Dale Carnegie, a pioneer in public speaking and personality development, believed that, "You can close more business in two months by becoming interested in other people than you can in two years by trying to get other people interested in you." Focus your attention on the person you are meeting. When you turn the spotlight away from yourself and shine it on others, they will bask in the glow. Ask the other person easy questions about himself: "Where are you from? What brought you to this event? How are you enjoying the event? What do you do for a living?" Perform a broad mini-interview and listen carefully to the answers. Your goal is to find something that you both have in common or something you both know about.

Larry King, one of the greatest television interviewers of all time, was once asked what makes a great conversationalist. His response: "The mark of a good conversationalist? Pay attention to what people say!" Too often, people are so concerned about the next thing they are going to say that they fail to listen. I truly believe this is where most people stumble. They want to appear smart or clever and are trying so hard to think of the perfect thing to say. Take your time and listen. Listening will help you more than any clever response because it will allow you to learn about the other person, which in turn will keep the conversation alive and vibrant.

Also, try divulging a little bit about yourself as you are talking. If the other person is listening, he may pick up on something to which he can relate. I often mention my children because so many business people have children, and it is easy to talk about children. I know others who mention their pets because there are so many animal lovers in the world. It often leads to an immediate connection. Think about something you enjoy that is common to many people and mention it during a conversation.

Remember, most of the people you will meet at a cocktail party won't have any idea of what to talk to you about either. Take control of the situation and make them feel comfortable. If you can't find anything in common, tell them it was nice to meet them and that you hope they enjoy the rest of the evening; then move on. If you are attending a business event that is designed for networking, simply say, "I don't want to dominate your time. Let's meet some other people. It was a pleasure meeting you."

Unless you make a strong connection, don't spend more than 12 minutes talking to a new acquaintance, or you may appear boorish.

Jump-start a Conversation

If you are trying to start a conversation and don't know where to begin, try some of the following questions or comments:

Example 1

Start with:

Where are you originally from?

Follow up with:

I understand that is a beautiful city.
What is the city best known for?
Do you still have family there?
Do you return for visits often?

Explore the city with them. If you know anyone from that city, or have visited there, discuss it.

Example 2

Start with:

Is this a busy time of the year for you?

Follow up with:

What do you do for a living?

Explore the various facets of the person's work.

Example 3

Start with:

What do you like to do when you are not working?

Follow up with questions related to hobbies, sports, or recreational activities.

If all else fails, talk about the weather. Just find some topic you are comfortable discussing and about which most people have some general knowledge.

Ask People for Advice

One of the nicest compliments that you can give a person is to ask them for advice or for their opinion. Try: "Do you know of a good restaurant in the area?" "Where is a good place to go shopping?" "After the conference, I have a few hours to kill before my flight. Do you have any recommendations as to what I could do during that time?" If you are both from out of town at a conference, ask the person, "Have you had time to see anything interesting in the city?"

Read the Newspaper

One way to keep a conversation alive is to discuss current events. Pick up a newspaper and scan it to see what's happening in the world. You always can say to a new acquaintance, "Wasn't that rescue attempt by the local paramedics something?" Or if you are at a conference in Minnesota, "Boy, the Twins have been playing well lately." Pick a couple of items that you think will be good conversation pieces and read them carefully. I know one man who really has no interest in sports, but he always reads the sports section before going to a party because many conversations inevitably turn to sports, and he wants to be able to participate. If you are going to be with a group that will likely talk about sports, read the sports page. If you will be with a group that will talk about business, scan the Wall Street Journal or surf the Internet. It doesn't take much time or effort to get up to speed on current events, and it might assist you in identifying a business opportunity.

One thing you want to be careful of is being a phony. Don't try to pass yourself off as someone you are not. When asked whether he was a sports fan, the non-sportsman would say, "No, but I try to stay abreast of what is going on." This is a simple and honest explanation.

Topics to Avoid

Although politics, sex, or religion are often interesting topics, they generally should be avoided when talking to new acquaintances. Gossip also should be avoided. Even though the person you meet may be interested, you are not building a foundation of trust for a long relationship. You might say something that easily can be taken out of context, or you could fail to fully express yourself, causing your new acquaintance to get the wrong impression of what you are saying and, in turn, you. If you get sucked into a conversation on a taboo subject, ask the person who started the conversation what he or she thinks and get a "read" on where they are coming from. Then decide whether you really want to get involved in the discussion. Sometimes it is better and safer just to politely change the subject or excuse yourself from the conversation.

I often am amazed at how complete strangers who are diametrically opposed will get into a philosophical discussion and think each will change the other's lifelong and dearly held opinions in the course of a 10-minute conversation. Most people who will talk openly about such subjects are not going to change their opinions overnight, so your effort is futile. Often the only thing you will accomplish is offending the person or a bystander who is listening to the conversation. This defeats your whole purpose of engaging the person in conversation in the first place and could cause you to lose a potential client or contact before you have established a relationship. Avoid such situations because they often become embarrassing.

Give Your Undivided Attention

As you probably already know, nothing is worse than trying to carry on a conversation with someone who is looking all around the room. If you are looking for someone in particular and you don't want to miss him, explain the situation to the person with whom you are talking and excuse your looking around. One prominent politician in my home state developed a reputation as someone who *always* was scouting the room while he was talking to someone during a social or business event. He appeared to be insincere in any conversation while he was on the lookout for someone he deemed to be more important or influential. That was hardly a good way to impress people whose trust he was seeking. And it's not a good way to develop relationships that could lead to new customers or clients. Sincerity matters.

Be Positive

People who are positive in their thinking and in their actions are magnets. They attract people naturally and are good at carrying on conversations because they make people feel good about themselves. A good attitude is contagious.

When you talk to people, put this positive principle to work in the way you ask questions. When you are talking to a woman, don't start your conversation with, "Do you work?" It is very sexist. Would you ask a man if he works? If you are at a conference, don't begin a conversation with, "That last speaker was terrible." Ask the person what she thought of the speaker. Call it political correctness or anything else, but starting a conversation with a new acquaintance on a positive note is very important. Think about how you frame questions, and put yourself in the place of the person who has to answer them. Are the questions demeaning, outdated, and insensitive, or are they positive conversation builders?

Don't Be Shy

Many people walk into a room of strangers and instantly turn into wallflowers. If the room is full of strangers, why do you have to be afraid? No one knows who you are! Walk up to people and introduce yourself. If there is someone in the room whom you want to meet, walk up to him, introduce yourself, and tell him that you have wanted to meet him for some time. He should be flattered by the compliment.

Generally, it is easiest to begin a conversation with a person standing alone because you are not interrupting an existing conversation. The next best option is to join a conversation involving three people. Why three people? It is easy to physically join the group. Conversations involving four or more people are more difficult to enter because the participants have formed a circle, and you have to break the circle to enter. That may be difficult and awkward. Conversations involving two people may be private or intimate, and an interruption may be unwelcome. You need to observe the participants' body language and intensity before interrupting. Conversations involving three participants are the place to start. You can approach the group with ease, and often at least one person in the group will be gracious and encourage your entry into the conversation.

When you enter the group, make sure that you shake everyone's hand. Begin with an introduction of yourself to the closest person. Don't go immediately to the person who you think may be the most important. That may offend the others.

If you are nervous about joining groups or meeting the popular people in the center of the room, begin with your fellow wallflowers. They will be grateful to have someone to talk to. In fact, you may have a great opportunity to start building a relationship because you each have something in common—shyness—and you will have their undivided attention.

Purpose of the Party

The purpose of most cocktail parties is not to eat and drink but rather to mingle. My law firm began a big marketing campaign and encouraged all of its associates to become more involved in trade associations, civic activities, and social gatherings. Fearing that their advancement would be stymied if they did not follow the directive, a group of associates decided to go to cocktail parties together. They were fun to watch. Immediately upon entering the room, they would go directly to the bar and then stand around and chat with each other regarding firm business for about 10 minutes. Next, they would fill not one but two plates of food at the hors d'oeuvres table and then sit down together at a table in the back of the room and eat, drink, and gossip the night away. They completely missed the opportunity presented by the event.

At first, meeting strangers is very difficult, but, with practice, you will become accustomed to it and actually may enjoy it. People are extremely interesting, and you can grow both personally and professionally by meeting different kinds of people. Remember the old saying: "A stranger is just a friend you haven't met yet."

Chapter VI

Making the Most of Any Event

*Opportunities multiply
as they are seized.
—Sun Tzu*

Business receptions, Rotary club meetings, golf tournaments, weddings, and parties are all fantastic opportunities to develop and use your rainmaking skills. Events such as these provide a "no-to-low" pressure setting for meeting people. If striking up a conversation is awkward for you, practice at a wedding. Talk to a stranger. You both have something in common—the bride and groom. If you can't remember names, practice at a friend's party. Use this as an opportunity to try to remember the names of all the people you meet.

Successful rainmakers seize all events to meet new people, increase their visibility, and establish credibility, all of which lead to developing relationships. Think about it. Over the course of your life, you likely have bought all sorts of goods or services from someone you met at an event. Think about where you met your insurance agent, accountant, stockbroker, or lawyer. The simple truth is that we all like to do business with people we know and with whom we feel comfortable. Successful rainmakers recognize this fact and capitalize on it. Most events are excellent forums for you to increase your visibility and begin the process of establishing credibility with people who can become lasting friends and business associates.

Guest Lists

For years, I was amazed at how one of the senior partners in my law firm always remembered the names of the spouses in the firm. He would see them only once a year at the firm retreat, but he instantly could recall their names. One day I asked him the secret to his uncanny ability to remember names. He grinned and said, "Each year before the firm retreat, I ask my secretary to obtain the names of all the spouses in the firm. For two days before the event, I read over them and memorize them." His system was easy and extremely effective. I have incorporated this practice with most events by requesting a list of attendees. Most event coordinators are more than happy to provide the list in advance of the event.

My recommendation is that before you go to any event, obtain a copy of the guest list and study it. If you recognize a name, highlight it, memorize it, and try to remember some small detail about the person, such as the topic of your last conversation, the person's interests, or something about the person's family. Write notes to yourself in the margins of the list so you can review the information a couple of times before you attend the event. You will find it much easier to recall information in the comfort of your office than when someone suddenly approaches you at an event and you frantically try to extract information from the now-idled memory bank of your brain.

Preparing in this fashion will give you the confidence to walk up to the person at the party, extend your hand, look her in the eye, and confidently greet her by name. It also will provide you with information to begin a conversation or to keep a conversation alive after you begin talking. The fact that you have remembered something personal about your acquaintance will also create a favorable impression, showing that you care about the person as an individual.

This technique can also help you meet people you don't know. If you see a person's name on the guest list you would like to meet, highlight the name, ask someone how to pronounce it correctly, and try to discover a little information about the person before the event. Friends, business associates, and co-workers, as well as industry and professional directories, are great resources for this information. Then, when you are at the event, make a point of introducing yourself or ask a friend or business acquaintance to introduce you. With the information you have gathered, you can initiate a conversation.

Peek at the Registration Desk

If you can't obtain a list of the attendees before the event, go to the event early and engage in some "reconnaissance." If nametags have been prepared for the event and are laid out on a table, take a few minutes to study them. If there are no nametags, introduce yourself to the receptionist as an invitee at the event and ask whether you can take a quick look at the guest list. You can tell the receptionist you are looking to see whether some of your acquaintances are going to be there. You will almost never be refused. In fact, often the receptionist will be a good source of information, and receptionists are usually happy to assist.

Meet New People

Before you go to an event, make a contract with yourself to meet and talk to a specific number of new people. Once you decide on the number of new people to meet, don't leave the event until you accomplish your goal. Start out slowly and realistically, based on your experience level. Meeting two new people at each event you attend is a good start. You can build from there. Remember, just saying your name and mumbling, "It's nice to meet you," does not count. You have to carry on a conversation during which you obtain valuable information about the person, and you must convey something memorable about yourself.

Survey the Room

When you enter a room in which an event is being held, move to the right or left out of pedestrian traffic and survey the room. Identify the location of the host and hostess, food, entertainment, and drinks. See whether you recognize anyone in the room and begin recalling their names.

Don't rush to the bar or to the hors d'oeuvre table. Good manners dictate that you greet the host and/or hostess first if they are available. After you have paid your respects, you may get drinks or sample the cuisine.

Avoid eating and drinking at the same time. It is very awkward to balance a plate in one hand and a drink in the other. Moreover, you want to keep your right hand available to shake hands.

Business Cards

Always carry your business cards with you and distribute them freely. Too many business people "save" their cards. But business cards are not like rare baseball cards. They don't become more valuable over time. In fact, their only value comes from handing them out, so always have some with you. Put a few in your wallet, purse, briefcase, golf bag, glove compartment, or any other convenient location and make a habit of giving them out frequently.

Some rainmakers make a habit of placing their business cards in their left pocket. This enables them to retrieve a card with their left hand while shaking hands with their right hand. Without fumbling, they can immediately retrieve their business cards. These same folks make a habit of placing the business cards they receive in their right pocket. This avoids mixing up the cards.

When you hand someone your business card, hand it to them flat so that the person can read the print. When you receive a business card, take a moment to read it. It will help you remember the person's name and can provide information to keep your conversation alive. In some cultures, it is a sign of respect to take several seconds to read the card. Never grab a person's card and stick it in your pocket without looking at it. That's rude.

While giving out business cards is important, it is more important to get business cards. Why? The odds of someone taking your business card and contacting you are low. If you get their business card, you can follow up with a note or e-mail.

Follow Up

After an event, record the names of the people you met along with a summary of your conversation or something you learned about them. For example:

> *Pete Riley:*
>
> *big Raiders fan, two children, one of whom is going to attend Yale next year.*

If possible, do that before you leave the event or on your way home. Don't have anything to write on? Use the person's business card. Don't wait until the next day when you are back in the office to write it down. You are likely to either forget to do it or to forget key information that should be recorded. Back at home or at your office, place the paper in a file designated to keep this sort of information or in a computer database. Eventually, your notes will become an invaluable database of names and personal information about your expanding list of acquaintances.

Offer to Help With Event Registration

If you are asked to help at an event, volunteer to work at the registration desk or the bar, the two places almost everyone at the event will visit. Of the two, the registration desk is the best place to work because you get to greet everyone and serve as a host of the event. You also will have the opportunity to introduce yourself and learn the names of those in attendance. In fact, you are now at an advantage because by being behind the registration desk you will be perceived as a person in the know.

The bar is a good place to work because most of the people in attendance will at some point become thirsty, and for some unknown reason people like to linger at bars and talk to bartenders. This offers a golden opportunity to strike up conversations.

Print Your Name Boldly

When you are attending an event where nametags are being worn by the attendees, make sure your name is printed in large, clear, bold letters. Avoid cursive and other hard-to-read writing. Printing with capital letters is best. You want to make it easy for people to read your name and learn it.

Nametags on the Right

Nametags always should be worn on the upper right side of your chest. Placing the nametag on the upper right side of your chest makes it much easier for people to see it because when you shake someone's hand, the nametag will be directly in front of her. Unfortunately, most people wear their nametags on their left side, over their heart. This is actually one of the hardest places for people to see it. When you extend your right hand to shake someone else's hand, your body naturally turns to the left, and a nametag positioned on your left chest turns away from the person you are meeting, defeating the whole purpose of wearing a nametag.

Likewise, a nametag worn low on your right side disappears under your arm when you extend your hand to meet someone. You want to make it easy, not awkward, for the person you are greeting to see—and remember—your name.

Women have a unique problem with nametags. They often cannot pin or clip a nametag on their clothing, and they struggle to find an appropriate place to put the tag. The best remedy for this problem is to purchase a chain with two clips on the ends that will grasp a nametag. This chain can be worn around the neck at an appropriate height.

If you keep the chain in your purse, it will always be available when you need it.

Know When to Say "When"

For some, the greatest challenge at an event is limiting the amount of alcohol they consume. The transition from college student to young professional is difficult at many levels, but knowing the appropriate amount to drink may be the most difficult. After a few drinks, young professionals, especially when in groups with their peers, often revert to collegiate norms.

It is fine to have a good time with your friends, but the line between being "social" and "drunk" is a fine one. Be extra careful when others are present. Don't get buzzed at cocktail parties or at weddings that superiors or potential clients may be attending. Although your fun persona may increase your visibility at the event, it may cost you credibility. People may be hesitant to trust you with important business affairs because of a perceived lack of maturity.

Company events also are potential pitfalls for young professionals. You feel comfortable in the company of your co-workers, and you tend to let down your guard. Not all of the guests there are indulging themselves and, at some point, the difference between your alcohol consumption and the consumption of others can become great. People don't only remember what you do between the hours of 9 to 5. They are constantly observing you. It is simply human nature. While it may never be expressed as an issue, outrageous or inappropriate behavior has the potential to linger in the back of people's minds. When a key assignment arises at work, your past behavior could be the deciding factor between you or a colleague receiving the project.

So, is the answer to never drink at an event? No. The answer is to know your limits on alcohol consumption. If you start to become goofy after three drinks, pace yourself and have only two drinks. If you want more, join your friends at a different location where supervisors, clients, and potential clients are not present.

Some of these ideas may seem obvious. Others may seem unnecessary. But maximizing opportunities to meet people and develop new relationships can lead to a more prosperous future. You may find greater comfort standing in the corner at a reception and talking to people you already know, but the person who is shaking hands, behaving appropriately, taking mental notes, making new acquaintances, and developing new relationships may find himself with a customer or client you could have had.

Why not use your time productively? Why not use your time to meet people whose lives you can enrich and who can enrich your life? Even if you don't find a new business deal at the next social function you attend, you may find a friend for a lifetime.

Chapter VII

Good Manners Matter

Your manners are always under examination, and by committees little suspected—a police in citizens' clothes—but are awarding or denying you very high prizes when you least think of it.
—Ralph Waldo Emerson

Good manners are extremely important, and they convey a strong first impression. Mastering manners will enable you to be confident in a variety of settings with people from all walks of life.

In the business world, dining out and attending after-hours business functions are integral parts of personal marketing. In fact, many deals and personal relationships are made at these types of events. The manner in which you behave speaks volumes about you. Keep in mind that people are evaluating you whether they are conscious of it or not. People who were reared in an environment where etiquette was constantly reinforced and practiced place a high value on good manners. These people, and others whom you will meet, form opinions based on your behavior on such occasions. Therefore, exercising proper business etiquette always is important.

After being elected student body president at the university I attended, I had the honor of being invited to a dinner hosted by the university president. I had no idea what to expect. When I arrived, I was overwhelmed. Never in my life had I seen so many forks, knives, spoons, plates, and wine glasses at one place setting. My anxiety level, which was already high, was raised several notches. I was in way over my head, and the sweat started beading on my forehead. It was one of the longest evenings of my life. (It took four hours to complete the meal!) From that night on, I knew that I had to become better versed in the social graces. Because I was so worried about making a fool of myself, I felt very uncomfortable and had a miserable evening. Looking back, if I had felt more at ease, it could have been one of the most exciting evenings of my life.

This chapter is intended to provide you with some basic information on business etiquette. You may not fully appreciate its value now, but when you find yourself in a formal setting, you will be glad you read it and hopefully memorized parts of it. In fact, before you go to a networking event, open the book and review this chapter. You always will feel more self-confident if you know the rules of the game.

Invitations

When you receive an invitation to an event that requests the favor of a reply (RSVP), you should always respond. It is discourteous not to do so. The manner in which you respond is dictated by the formality of the invitation. If someone leaves a message on your answering machine inviting you to dinner, it is appropriate to respond by telephone. If you receive a formal written invitation without a phone number to reply, you should reply in writing. The following is an appropriate reply to a formal invitation:

> ***Mr. and Mrs. John Doe (accept with pleasure / regret that they cannot accept) the kind invitation of Mr. and Mrs. William Deem for Saturday, June 23, 2009, at seven o'clock, Pittsburgh.***

Some invitations will enclose a reply card similar to the following:

> *M* _____ *will* _____
>
> *attend the Governor's reception on*
> *Saturday, June 23, 2009,*
> *at seven o' clock.*

If you receive such a reply card, it should be completed in one of two ways. If you can attend:

> *Mr. and Mrs. John Doe will attend the Governor's reception on Saturday, June 23, 2009, at seven o'clock.*

If you are unable to attend:

> *Mr. and Mrs. John Doe will be unable to attend the Governor's reception on Saturday, June 23, 2009, at seven o'clock.*

Be sure to reply on behalf of all the people to whom the invitation was addressed. If, as in the example, Mr. and Mrs. John Doe are invited, respond on behalf of both of them, not just one of them.

For formal events and sit-down dinners, you should arrive on time or no later than 15 minutes after the scheduled time.

Formal Dinners

A formal place setting on an elegant table can be very intimidating if you are not accustomed to formal dining. As you learn the "rules" of dining, your anxiety level will drop, and you will be able to appreciate the elegance before you. A brief explanation of the location and purpose of the plates and silverware at a typical dinner will eliminate any fears you may have.

Plates

The largest dish in your place setting is the service plate or charger. Its purpose is to serve as a base for other dishes served throughout the meal; therefore, it will remain on the table for most of the meal. The wait staff will place the dishes for the other courses on it and remove the dishes from it when you are finished. You never eat from this plate.

To your far left and above the fork is your bread plate. It is a small plate whose name implies its purpose: to hold your butter, bread, and rolls. It is important to remember the placement of this plate because if you use the wrong one, you will throw off everyone else at the table. If you are in doubt, pass the rolls to the person next to you and follow her lead.

Finally, your salad either will be placed on the charger or on a plate to the right of the bread plate, but still to the left of the charger.

Your waiter will remove the various plates and silverware at the appropriate times. Wait for the waiter to remove the plates. It is poor form to push away your plate.

Silverware

A formal place setting often contains numerous forks, spoons, and knives. When trying to decide which to use, there is a very easy rule to follow. Work from the outside in. For example, the first fork that you will need to use will be the fork farthest from your plate on the left. The first spoon will be the farthest one from the plate on the right. With each course, work your way through the silverware from the farthest from the plate to the closest to the plate. If you find a spoon and a fork placed horizontally across the top of your plate, don't panic. This silverware is for dessert!

Should you accidentally drop a piece of silverware on the floor during the dinner, don't pick it up, wipe it off with your napkin, and use it. Ask the waiter for a new piece and continue with the meal.

Finally, remember that silverware is to be used for eating. Forks and spoons are not toys to be played with at the table. Don't pick them up and tap them on the table or use them as a toothpick. Hanging spoons from your face may entertain the children, but it won't amuse your boss or your client.

Napkins

You usually will find your napkin either to the left of your place setting or on your plate. Generally, when you sit down at the table you should place the napkin in your lap even if no food is present yet. If you get up and leave the table during the meal, place the napkin to the left of your plate. If you forget which side to place your napkin, fold it and place it on your chair. Your napkin should remain on your lap until you are ready to leave the table. When you leave, place your unfolded napkin on the table in front of you if all of the plates have been removed or to the right if the plates remain.

Napkins should be used to remove food particles from your face and fingers. They are not to be used for cleaning your eye glasses, wiping your nose, or other unseemly activities.

Community Food

On your table, you often will find "community food," such as salad dressings, butter, bread, or rolls. This food should be shared with everyone. If it is in front of your place setting, you are in charge of passing it to others. For example, if the bread basket is in front of you, pick it up, hold the bread basket in one hand and remove a roll with the other hand. Avoid touching other pieces of bread. After you take a piece, offer the bread to the person on your left and then pass it to your right. The general rule is "offer to the left, pass to the right."

If you are the person receiving the bread and you do not want any, continue to pass it on to others. Don't set it down on the table or refuse it when passed to you. It is a courtesy to your dinner companions to pass the bread or any other community food around the table.

After you select a piece of bread or a roll, place it on your bread dish. Tear off a piece that is no bigger than two bites worth, and eat that piece before tearing off another. If butter is served, place butter on each piece just before you eat it. Don't take a big bite out of the center of the roll and set the remainder on the bread plate.

Soup

Properly eating soup can be a bit counterintuitive. Instead of dipping the spoon in the bowl and bringing it toward you, you should move the spoon away from you. The reason for this is simple. If you draw the spoon toward you, you are more likely to spill it on yourself.

When the soup is almost finished, it is acceptable to slightly tilt the bowl *away* from yourself and get the last spoonfuls. When you are finished, place your spoon to the side so the waiter knows you are finished.

When to Begin Eating

You should never begin eating until everyone at the table is served or returns from the buffet table. Moreover, you should wait until the host or hostess begins to eat or signals that it is appropriate to begin.

"See-food"

Don't talk when food is in your mouth. This habit appears unsightly to the people who are looking at you and sounds disgusting to those who are listening to you. Be courteous to those with whom you are dining; don't ask questions right after they put food in their mouth or ask so many questions that they never have an opportunity to eat their meal.

Finger Foods

What can you eat with your fingers? Bread, cookies, chips, crispy fries (thick-cut steak fries may require a fork), nuts, pickles, and most foods that could be served as hors d'oeuvres. A general rule of thumb is this: If they make a mess when you pick them up, use a fork or spoon. Just use your best judgment and avoid making an unsightly mess. And don't lick your fingers!

Other Tips

Turn your cell phone off. Text messaging and talking on the phone during a meal is not multi-tasking. It is rude.

Don't return to a buffet table with a dirty plate. It is unsanitary. Discard your plate and obtain a clean one.

Discard toothpicks from hors d'oeuvres in an appropriate manner. Don't litter the serving table with them or place them back on the serving tray. You should place them on your plate, roll them up in a napkin and dispose of them later, or deposit them on a tray designated for dirty dishes. Do not chew on them or use them to pick your teeth.

Never "double dip." When a sauce or dip is served, dip only the cracker, shrimp, vegetable, or chip in the dip one time. Do not dip anything back into a sauce after you have taken a bite from it, and do not turn it around and dip the other end.

Don't order messy foods like spaghetti that can splash. Be careful when biting into cherry tomatoes, puff pastries, and hot hors d'oeuvres. They can splatter on the people with whom you are talking.

When removing food from your mouth, the general rule is that you should remove it the same way it went in. What goes in with a fork should come out with a fork. If you discover a piece of bone in a bite of chicken, return it to your plate by way of the fork. Fish is an exception. You may remove tiny fish bones from your mouth with your fingers. Placing them on a fork is simply too difficult.

When asked to "please pass the salt," pick up *both* the salt and pepper and place them on the table within reach of the person next to you. That person will, in turn, pass both to the next person until they reach the person who requested them. If you

are passing them, don't use them when they are in your posses-
sion. Wait until the person requesting them is finished and then
request them for yourself.

Little Tests

You may be thinking, "What's the big deal? Who is ever going to judge me based on how I eat a meal?" All I can say is that
you will be surprised. During interviews and other circumstances
when I have been evaluated for a position, my table etiquette
has been tested. The most common test has been the salt and
pepper test. The person making the request for salt waits to see
whether you pass both the salt and the pepper. How did I know
that I was being tested? The requester barely used the salt after
receiving it.

Take the time to improve your social skills. It will serve you
well and may build credibility in certain relationships.

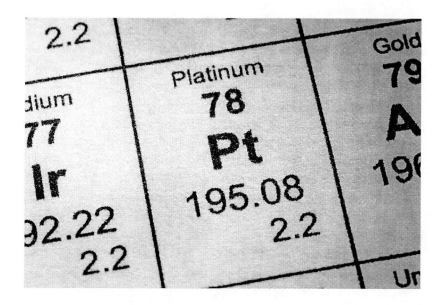

Chapter VIII

Follow the Platinum Rule

Always do right — this will gratify
some and astonish the rest.
—Mark Twain

We all were taught the "Golden Rule" in elementary school. "Do unto others as you would have them do unto you." Well, forget the Golden Rule. In today's business world, it does not apply. The "Platinum Rule" governs. "Do unto others as they want to be done unto!" In other words, don't treat your clients the way *you* would expect to be treated. Treat them the way *they* expect to be treated. Your goal should be to meet and exceed *their* expectations, not your expectations!

Everything in today's society is designed for speed, convenience, and instant gratification. People no longer have to do their banking during regular business hours. They can bank online and receive cash from a machine. Investors no longer have to place stock and bond orders through a broker. They simply can strike the keyboards of their personal computers and place an or-der in minutes. Taxpayers no longer need an accountant because they can buy software to do their taxes.

With all of these advances in technology, people now have heightened expectations regarding everything, including personal services. If service providers are going to survive the competition against machines, they must provide a service that a computer or a machine can't match or duplicate.

The one thing a computer cannot do is maintain a relation-ship. A computer program cannot hold a client's hand in times of crises, provide sage advice, or exceed expectations. People who provide their clients these personal touches will always prosper.

With this in mind, everything you say and do should be ex-ternally focused. What does the client want and need? If you ask that question throughout the day and act on the answer, you will live the "Platinum Rule."

This chapter provides you with ideas and techniques to meet your customers' expectations.

Return Telephone Calls Promptly

An easy and inexpensive way to impress your clients is to return their calls promptly. Develop a personal contract with yourself to return telephone calls within 24 hours or less of their receipt. Let your clients and customers know their business prob-lems or needs are important to you. They will love you for this one simple act.

If you can't return the phone call during regular business hours, call after hours and leave a message or send an e-mail. Many companies and individuals have answering services, a Blackberry, or voice mail. The important thing is to make an ef-fort to contact them.

For example, if Jim Sims called while you were out of the of-fice and you didn't get back in the office until after 5 p.m., don't assume that he has left work. Try calling him even if it is unlikely that you will reach him. If the purpose for the call is important to Jim, he still may be waiting for your call. If it is not important, you can leave a message or call back the next day. "Jim, I'm returning your call. I tried to reach you at 6 p.m. on Wednesday, but no one answered. I will call back in the morning." This message lets Jim know you were concerned about his problem, made an effort to return his call promptly, will try to reach him again at a specific time—and that you work hard.

Flatter your clients by letting them know the extremes to which you will go to return their calls. For example, if you are traveling, send an e-mail or leave a message such as, "John, I'm sorry I missed your call. I'm in Atlanta today and am leaving for my return flight in five minutes. I will be back in the office tomorrow morning and will call you then."

This short message explains why you didn't return the call earlier without going into unnecessary detail, conveys to the caller that you have made an extra effort to return his call, and provides a reasonable estimate of when you will call back. The important thing is that your client knows you are trying to meet his expectations.

Be Prepared

The Boy Scouts' motto is right on point: "Always be prepared." Organization and preparedness convey a sense of strength and control and go a long way toward establishing credibility in your relationship with a client.

Preparedness is important both when you meet with a client and when you talk to a client on the telephone. When you meet with a client, be ready to discuss his problems and offer solutions or options. Likewise, before returning a phone call, try to anticipate the caller's needs and be ready to act. At a minimum, you should have the caller's file or account information in front of you before you return the call. That will enable you to refresh your memory and answer basic questions. Your client will appreciate the attention and the respect you are demonstrating by not wasting his valuable time.

A few years ago, a busy young lawyer in a large firm learned this lesson the hard way. He was assigned a case involving a college, and the president of the college requested a meeting to discuss the status of the matter. The associate grabbed the file on his way out of the office and made just a cursory review of its contents. During the course of the meeting, it became apparent to the college president that the associate was not abreast of the file and that the meeting was a waste of time. A few days later, the president of the college called the managing partner of the firm and said, "I realize the importance of a lawyer's time, and I am willing to pay a fair hourly rate for that time. But the lawyers in your firm have to realize that although I do not charge for my services by the hour, my time is also valuable." A point well made.

This example proves two important points. First, we have a responsibility to our clients to be prepared and to value their time. Second, good client relationships are invaluable. How many clients would take the time to voice their concern or frustration or even feel comfortable doing so? Either strong lines of communication existed between the college and the law firm, or a good rapport existed between the president and the managing partner. Regardless, the law firm was fortunate the president called. Most clients won't complain. They will just take their business elsewhere.

Here's another example of preparedness. Tom, a life insurance agent, was asked to submit a life insurance proposal for several key officers and directors of a large company. From the request for proposals, Tom knew what the company wanted, but he wanted to know what the company *needed*. During conversations with company employees, Tom gathered key information, including information about his competitors.

Tom and three other agents were asked to make presentations to the board. The agents for the other companies submitted 30-page outlines detailing their proposals to each board member. Tom submitted one page. He gave the detailed information to the person who issued the request for proposals. On his one sheet, Tom addressed what the company wanted, compared his product to the offerings of the other companies, and explained to the board what they *needed*.

Later in the day, a board member called Tom and invited him to return to the board room. He was advised that his proposal was selected. During the course of the conversation, the chairman said, "I suppose that we will need to schedule physicals for everyone." Tom replied, "Sir, your physical is scheduled for Monday morning, and I will be present to walk you through it, and the physicals of the other officers are scheduled for later in the week." The chairman looked at Tom and said, "Wasn't it a bit presumptuous of you to schedule physicals before you were awarded the contract?" "No sir," Tom responded, "it is easier to cancel a physical than to schedule one."

The chairman sat in silence for a moment and said, "I knew we picked the right person." The chairman and the board members became one of Tom's best referral sources for the remainder of his career.

Tom was right on the mark. He gathered information and insight from friends within the organization, made a presentation that differentiated himself from the competition, gave the board added value by determining what products they really needed, and exceeded the board's expectations by anticipating their needs. If you follow Tom's approach, success will rain on you.

Don't Over-anticipate

While it is important to be prepared, don't let it paralyze you. Don't always presume you know why the client is calling. Often people get a phone message and delay returning the call because they assume they know what the caller wants. "Joe must be calling about the results of the audit. We won't be finished with that until next week. I'll call him back then." Don't put your client off. Return the call and be prepared to update the client. Keeping your clients informed is a big part of your job. No one likes surprises. Many mediocre professionals have prospered because they did the one thing that the "superstars" failed to do—they developed personal relationships with their clients and kept their clients informed. In doing so, you might even be surprised. Your client may be calling to give you more business or a good referral. Never hesitate to be responsive. Regular contact is as important to your client as having the answer.

There are three important things to remember: 1) You are not clairvoyant; 2) your clients pay you to be responsive in a timely manner; and 3) bad news does not get better with time. Remember, your client has a right to know the status of her account and, if you don't keep her abreast of her account, someone in another firm will.

Service Means Business

The way we treat and care for our customers often determines whether we keep them and even expand our relationship with them. Here are some tried and true tips to maintain and develop relationships.

Be prompt. Clients will be impressed if you can deliver on time, and they will become clients for life if they know they can count on you.

Do not over-promise, but do establish deadlines. Your clients have high expectations of you. Don't turn those high expectations into unrealistic expectations by making promises you can't possibly keep. Find out what your client's expectations are and be realistic about your ability to deliver. If the client is unrealistic, let him know, but offer a realistic alternative. Don't simply say, "Sorry, I can't do it by then." Explain why you can't do it and offer a realistic time frame. Often a middle ground exists. You may lose some business in the short term, but you ultimately will build credibility. Moreover, you will reduce your stress level by taking this approach. Good, honest communication with your clients is essential to maintaining long-lasting relationships.

Provide project updates. Immediately advise clients and colleagues at work when you are falling short of a deadline. Nothing is worse than telling a person that a project is not complete on the date it is due, especially when you knew days in advance. If a problem develops, report it immediately. Most people will appreciate the call and, if they can, will give you an extension. Work with them to find a solution. Don't wait until the last minute and make it their problem to solve. Be a problem solver.

Keep your clients involved in decision-making. If you have a "hands-on" client, make sure you keep her involved in the decision-making. Let her know days in advance when a decision has to be made and advise her of her options. Don't wait until the last minute. If you have a client who is not "hands on" and who relies heavily on you, don't unilaterally make all of the decisions. Try to engage the client in the decision-making process. Make him feel as if he truly is participating in the decision-making even if you really are making all of the decisions. That goes a long way in maintaining a relationship.

Give bad news as well as good. Everyone likes to call a client to give the good news. Nobody likes to call a client to give bad news. However, it is very important for you to give the client both good news and bad news promptly. As stated earlier, bad news seldom improves with age. Your client has a right to know everything about his matters in a timely manner. Personally conveying bad news ensures that the information is properly and accurately relayed to the client, and, second, it lets the client know that you are behind him in good times and bad. Giving bad news is hard to do, but it earns respect and solidifies relationships.

Know your client. Always know your client and your client's business. You can learn more about your client through numerous sources: Talk to friends, employees of the company, and business colleagues; obtain information from the chamber of commerce; request annual reports if your client is publicly traded; search old newspapers and magazines; review courthouse records; or go online and search the Internet. A wealth of information is out there for your use. Find it and use it. Your clients will be impressed that you took the time to learn more about them.

Listen to your clients. I cannot emphasize that enough. Your clients are the greatest source for the information you need to be successful. Ask them questions and listen to their answers carefully. You will identify problems faster and solve them more quickly. Moreover, you may identify additional business opportunities for your firm. For example, elderly people often go to lawyers to have a will prepared. They think a will is all they need to properly prepare for their retirement and death. A good lawyer will take the time to talk to a client to determine what that individual's real needs are. Perhaps the client needs a trust established, a durable power of attorney, or an advance health care directive prepared in the event he becomes incapacitated. If the lawyer does not take the time to ask the appropriate questions and listen to the answers, he is failing to serve his client, and he is missing an opportunity to provide a full range of legal services.

Be a problem-solver. When you develop a reputation for being a problem-solver, customers will beat a path to your door. Clients want to turn over their problems to people who can relieve their burden. Too many professionals tell clients what their problems are without offering any advice or guidance to solve them. From the client's perspective, his burden has just become greater, and why would he pay big dollars to a professional who makes his life more difficult?

When a client has a problem, make it *your* problem and offer ideas and alternatives to solve it. Successful rainmakers use problem-solving as a mechanism to cross-sell services within their firms or to refer business to other professionals in the community. If you are handling a corporate matter for a client and you identify an insurance need, offer to help find an insurance agent for your client. You are helping your client solve a problem, and who knows? Someday that agent may reciprocate the referral. Both you and your client can benefit from problem-solving.

Your goal is to become the easiest and most helpful person your client works with.

Chapter IX

Making the Most
of a Presentation

The truth isn't the truth until people believe you,
and they can't believe you if they don't know what you're saying,
and they can't know what you're saying if they don't listen to you,
and they won't listen to you if you're not interesting,
and you won't be interesting unless you say things
imaginatively, originally, freshly.
—William Bernbach

As professionals, we often are called upon to address civic and professional groups and to present ideas and products to clients. These presentations are an excellent opportunity to gain visibility as well as credibility, the cornerstone of building a relationship. Every presentation, no matter how big or small, should be taken seriously. And because we instantly are judged when we speak, it is very important to develop strong and effective communication skills. Good communicators are perceived as intelligent, confident, and knowledgeable. Because they have the same qualities that attract business, good public speakers often are good rainmakers.

Know Your Audience

The first rule in public speaking is to know your audience. Who will be listening to you? Will your audience be fellow professionals or potential clients? Will they be senior citizens, Baby Boomers, or members of Generation X? What is the socioeconomic class of the audience? Does your audience know anything about the topic on which you are going to speak? What does the audience need or expect from your presentation?

Knowing the answers to these types of questions is critical to a successful presentation. You cannot effectively communicate a message to an audience that you know nothing about. The content of your remarks must fit the audience's knowledge base and needs. Choose language and examples to which your audience can relate. Don't talk about $500,000 homes when the majority of your audience makes $25,000 a year. Don't use references to modern pop culture if your audience is older than 50. Think about ways to relate to your audience.

When you accept a speaking engagement, ask the person extending the invitation at least three questions: (1) What is the typical profile of the audience; (2) what is the size of the audience; and (3) why are they interested in hearing me speak on this topic? Typically, you'll want to ask more questions, but these three will get you started and will help you prepare your strategy.

Too often speakers don't know their audience. As a result, speakers either assume the audience knows nothing about their topic, and the presentation is so basic that it insults the audience's intelligence, or they speak over the audience's head and use acronyms (abbreviations for words and phrases) and terminology unfamiliar to the audience.

In addition to knowing his audience's basic profile, a good speaker watches his audience. When you see blank stares, puzzled expressions, or restlessness in your audience, you likely have presentation problems. If that happens, think quickly and re-engage your audience. Before arriving at your speaking engagement, think about slight changes you can make during the presentation that won't throw you out of sync. Then, if you sense that you are losing your audience, ask questions of the audience. This is an effective way to re-engage the audience. Preparing an alternative plan before you begin speaking can be comforting if things start to go awry.

Keep the Message Simple

Public speaking is easier when you have a clear, concise, and simple message. It is easier for you and easier for the audience. Try to think of one or two sentences that sum up the idea you are trying to convey, and think of it days *before* you begin to speak. Waiting until the day of your presentation is too late to devise your theme and may cause you to appear unsure of yourself and your topic—not something you want to convey to potential clients.

Poor speakers often end a disjointed presentation by hesitating for a moment and saying, "I guess the point of my talk is...." If you don't know what the point of your presentation is before you begin to speak, you have no business speaking in the first place. Deliver your speech in a clear and consistent manner from beginning to end.

During the 1992 presidential campaign, the Clinton presidential committee mastered this principle. Hanging on the wall of Bill Clinton's campaign office was a sign that read, "It's the economy, stupid." The message was clear, simple, and to the point. To win the election, Clinton had to stay focused on the key issue of the economy and deliver the message consistently. It worked for him, and it can work for you.

Avoid Technical Terms and Acronyms

C.H.O.W. What does that mean? It is business jargon for "Change of Ownership." Many speakers misjudge the sophistication of their audiences and use terms and phrases that most members of the audience don't know or that are unfamiliar. If you must use acronyms and technical phrases, take time to explain what they are and what they mean. You likely are speaking to educate your audience, and this is part of the process.

Control Body Language

As a speaker, you send both verbal and nonverbal messages to your audience. The way you stand, gesticulate, and move during your presentation sends messages. These messages either enhance your presentation or detract from it.

There are a few important things to remember about body language. First, strong eye contact with your audience is important. You can use eye contact to make everyone in your audience feel involved in the presentation. Look at people in different areas of the room. Don't focus on one person or one area of the room. If you are uncomfortable looking at people when you speak, try looking at objects above and behind the audience, such as clocks, signs, or doors. Audience members will perceive that you are looking at them. Additionally, this will force you to look up and away from your notes. Eventually, you will become more comfortable and confident, and you can begin looking directly into the eyes of audience members.

Second, stand up straight. Don't lean on the podium or slouch over it. Such behavior suggests that your message is unimportant. Many speakers use the podium as a crutch. On some occasions, slouching or leaning can be used to emphasize a point, but generally it is bad form.

Third, gesticulate. Use your arms and hands to emphasize important points in your message. When you practice your speech, add gestures so they become natural and do not appear forced. Once again, movement helps to keep the audience's attention.

Finally, think about where your body is. Many effective speakers occasionally move away from the podium while they are speaking to remove the barrier between themselves and their audience and to keep the audience's attention. Whenever I see the audience is getting bored, I move away from the podium or to the other side of the stage. Movement grabs their attention. If the people on the left side of the room are nodding off, I walk over in their direction. Cordless microphones are wonderful because they allow you to be a part of the audience. Use them whenever you have the opportunity. If there isn't a cordless microphone, walk away from the podium and raise your voice. The variety and movement will recapture the audience.

Here are some additional tips for captivating your audience:

Modulate your voice tone. Good public speakers raise and lower their voices to add interest to their presentation and to emphasize particular points. Lowering your voice to a whisper can capture the attention of an audience as effectively as shouting the point. Voice tone is to a speaker what a musical score is to a movie. You can use the tone of your voice to emphasize points and to evoke the emotions of the audience. The great civil rights leader Martin Luther King, Jr. was a master at using voice tone to captivate and excite his audiences. Make a conscious effort to raise and lower your voice. Try varying your tone when preparing for your next presentation. You will be pleasantly surprised to see how your audience reacts.

Pause occasionally. Pausing can add drama to a presentation as well. It gives the audience time to reflect on your message, and it gives you time to catch your breath. Don't race through your presentation. Both you and the audience will be better off.

Invite audience participation. The best way to keep an audience's attention and to help it learn the material you are presenting is to involve its members in the presentation. There is an old Chinese proverb:

Tell me, and I'll forget.
Show me, and I may remember.
Involve me, and I'll understand.

When you prepare your remarks, try thinking of ways to involve your audience. Ask yourself: What would interest me if I were sitting in the audience?

One way to involve the audience is by developing "case scenarios" or hypotheticals. Prepare a written, hypothetical example of a problem that your presentation is going to address and distribute it to the audience. From this, you can have a question-and-answer session or a group discussion. Moreover, preparing the scenarios will force you to think about the composition of your audience and assist you in formulating the delivery of your message.

Take, for example, a financial planner who wants to market his services through speaking engagements in the community.

Most of the people in his town have heard financial planners speak before. How can he distinguish himself from the rest? Rather than lecturing the group for 20 minutes about stocks, bonds, taxes, and diversification—*yawn*—he could begin his presentation with a brief introduction of the services he offers, highlight the points he wants the audience to remember, and present a few relevant case scenarios. It is very important for him to know his audience when he is developing the scenarios. If he is addressing a group of senior citizens, his case scenario likely would involve a person in his late 60s facing issues involving retirement income, long-term care, estate planning, etc. If the financial planner is talking to 40-year-olds, the case scenarios likely would include hypothetical examples that address preparing for a child's education, income tax deferrals, and saving for retirement.

When you develop case scenarios, think of the questions you frequently are asked or problems that you frequently encounter. Combine those experiences with advice you want the audience to remember when it leaves the presentation. This combination can be very powerful. But remember to be careful not to use scenarios that can identify a client. No one wants his or her mistakes highlighted for an audience. Discretion and common sense are always important.

Another technique that I use when asked to speak for an hour or longer on a dry subject is to offer prizes to the audience for correct answers, good questions, and general participation. This can be a lot of fun. The "prizes" can be anything. Usually the simpler and less expensive the better. Candy, coffee mugs, or pens with your company logo are great. You will be amazed at the increased participation. People like to win prizes no matter what they are. Once again, you need to know your audience before you prepare. If you are speaking to a group of no-nonsense business executives, don't use the "prize" approach. However, if you are talking to a civic group or a group of senior citizens, give it a try.

Involving your audience in the presentation will not only create a better learning experience for them, it will be more fun and interesting for you. When you are comfortable and enjoying yourself, it will show in the quality of your presentation.

Questions and Answers

Near the beginning of your speech, let the audience know how you will address questions. Do you want the audience to ask questions during your presentation, or do you want to take questions at the end? This will depend greatly on the amount of time you have, the amount of material you want to cover, the size of your audience, and your ability to be interrupted and regain your train of thought. If you have plenty of time to make your presentation and are comfortable fielding questions, let the audience ask questions as you speak. Often you will get more participation. However, one audience member with his or her own agenda can throw off your whole presentation, so if you are on a tight time frame and have a lot of material to cover, save questions for the end. If you tell the audience that you will take questions at the end of your presentation, make sure you leave time for questions. You want to maintain credibility with your audience.

Always be courteous to questioners. It will encourage questions from the audience. Thank audience members for asking questions. Let them know when they ask a good question. "Thank you, that's a great question." "Your question leads me into my next point, thank you." Positive reinforcement will encourage others to ask questions. Don't ever embarrass a person who asks a question. Sometimes speakers will crack a little joke about a question or tease a questioner. While this may get a laugh from the audience, it may hinder a hesitant or shy person from asking a question. Reward all questions with positive reinforcement.

When you receive a question, summarize it and repeat it. This practice keeps your audience informed and gives you a few extra seconds to formulate an answer. Moreover, address the entire audience when you answer the question, not just the person who asked the question. This practice keeps the entire audience engaged. When you have several questions in a row and answer each questioner directly, you will lose your audience quickly.

Occasionally, you will receive a hostile question. When this occurs, try to deflect the question. "I'll be covering that subject in a few minutes." "Please see me after the presentation." Always remain calm and thank the questioner for asking the question. A positive response to a hostile question will build your stature with the audience.

Don't be afraid of question-and-answer sessions. As you prepare for your speech, think of questions that may arise. Ask a friend to "grill" you. Practice will boost your confidence. If you don't know the answer to a question, tell the audience. Don't fake it. Offer to research the issue and to report back to them at a later date. If it is a diverse group that will never be assembled again, ask those audience members who are interested in the answer to leave a business card and promise to e-mail them with the answer. What a great way to have follow-up contact.

Questions also are a good opportunity to reinforce key points you made during your presentation. "That question really highlights the point we discussed at the beginning of the presentation, which was _____. Thank you."

Question-and-answer sessions also are great opportunities to learn what is on the minds of your clients and potential clients. Store this information in the back of your mind and use it when preparing for future presentations or client sales calls.

Handouts

Distribute written materials that enhance your presentation. Most people learn in one of two ways—orally or visually. Your presentation will take care of the people who learn by hearing information, but it may not help those who learn by seeing. Handouts are perfect for the visual learners in the audience.

There are four important things to remember about handouts. First, their physical appearance should be neat and visually appealing. You want to make a good impression with the reader, and you want to stimulate the reader to look at the information. Second, the information should be clear and accurate. Accuracy is extremely important. Do not disseminate information you have not checked to ensure accuracy. In addition to losing credibility with a potential client, providing incorrect or misleading information could lead to a lawsuit.

Third, don't give your knowledge away for free. If you are making presentations to develop business, don't tell people at a free seminar how to solve their problems without your assistance. Create materials that highlight the issues and encourage audience members to call you for assistance. Don't "educate" yourself out of business. Finally, always include your name, company name, e-mail address, and telephone number on all of your handout materials. You want to make it easy for people to contact you for assistance.

Charts, Slides, and Graphics

You can make your presentation more interesting by using visual aids. An audience daydreams if its members have to listen to a talking head for any amount of time. A good rule of thumb is that you should not talk for more than 12 minutes at a time without introducing some type of visual aid. You can hold up the product you are selling, write on a chalk board, present slides, or play a video, but you should do something. Remember, the average person's attention span is very short.

Your visual aids should be varied. Don't just take excerpts from your speech and place them on a slide. Be creative. Illustrate the points you want to make with graphs, charts, photographs, and artwork. Mix up the types of graphics you use in your presentation to add interest. Visual aids will not only entertain your audience, they will also help your audience learn. As discussed earlier, many people are visual learners. They have to see something to remember it, and visual aids greatly assist them.

More tips:

Don't talk to the screen. Some speakers who use slides or computer-generated graphics look at the screen when they are talking and have their backs to the audience. Avoid this practice. The audience may not be able to hear because the speaker's voice is being projected in the wrong direction, and looking at someone's back becomes very boring. You want to face the audience as much as possible.

If you are using some type of a pointer, such as a laser pointer, be careful. Speakers with these types of devices tend to face the screen with greater frequency.

Don't read your speech. It's boring. Nothing will put an audience to sleep faster. If you are uncomfortable making a presentation, write your speech out on a piece of paper and practice it several times. Revise it until you are using familiar words and phrases, and don't try to be someone else.

Once you are comfortable with the flow of your speech, practice it aloud without looking at the paper. Highlight the areas where you get stuck and the important information you want the audience to remember. From these highlights, prepare notes that outline your speech. Don't write down too much information. Inexperienced speakers often write their entire speech on note cards. This is not a good practice because you will become dependent on the cards and simply read your speech, thereby forgetting to look at the audience when you speak. Only write down the bare essentials that will jog your memory, such as main topics, important dates, key phrases, and important statistics. You should be comfortable enough with what you are talking about to move into the next point with a quick glance at your paper.

Practice your presentation before you deliver it. This will improve your performance and reduce your anxiety. Stand in front of a mirror and deliver your presentation aloud a couple of times. You may find that a speech that looks great on paper sounds awkward when spoken aloud. If you become bored with your speech as you practice, make changes to it. Try to make it interesting. Vary your voice tone and add case scenarios or visual aids to the presentation. Do something to spice it up.

Also, remember to secure your notes. I learned this lesson the hard way. Once, when I was approaching the podium to speak, I dropped all of my note cards on the floor. They went everywhere. They were not numbered, and I had to fumble around trying to get them in order. I can imagine what the audience must have been thinking. Worse yet, I was shaken. My confidence was shattered. I just wanted to finish the speech and leave the stage. But from every bad experience, there is a lesson to be learned. Now I never go to the podium without my notes numbered and secured.

I recommend placing speech notes in large, bold letters on 8½ x11 sheets of paper and placing them in a three-ring binder. The three-ring binder keeps everything in order and looks professional when you are approaching and leaving the podium. (Also, it is more difficult to lose or drop a binder than note cards.) That works well for me, but you should use whatever system makes the most sense for you.

Record yourself. If you are new at public speaking or feel you need feedback, try tape recording or videotaping one of your speeches—not a practice session, but the actual speech. You may be surprised at what you find. Nervousness can manifest itself in some pretty annoying habits that you don't realize you have until you actually hear yourself speak.

I once had a teacher who always said "OK" when she paused to think. The habit was very distracting. Similarly, I recently attended a seminar in which a speaker said "umm" every time he paused for a breath. An hour of "umms" was maddening. A friend of mine who also attended the seminar said that he became so obsessed with the speaker's nervous habit that he quit listening to the message and started counting how many times the speaker said "umm" during a 10-minute period. I'm sure the speaker had no idea that he had such a habit, but if he had recorded himself it would have been—umm—clear as a bell. Take the time to record yourself to see what little annoying habits you may possess, and then work to correct them. You also can check your body language and tone of inflection. You will be a better speaker if you do it.

Use humor wisely. People learn better and enjoy themselves more when they are amused and relaxed. You can put your audience at ease by adding a little humor to your presentations. You don't need to be a comedian, and you have to determine for yourself whether you are good at telling stories, jokes, or other humorous anecdotes. Short, funny stories about yourself are best. Self-depreciating humor is often the safest route to go because you are making fun of yourself and no one else. Never make fun of someone in the audience. Others may laugh, but in the back of their minds they may worry about being the brunt of your next joke.

Humor, of course, is in the eye of the beholder. Once again, you have to know your audience. A politician recently told me that he developed a one-liner that was getting big laughs throughout the southern part of his state. When he delivered the line in the north, there was no response. It bombed. What was the difference? In the south, the subject had been on the front page of the newspapers for weeks, and in the north the story was on page five. The northern audience had no context for the joke. Know your audience.

You also have to be very careful not to go over the edge and offend someone. Avoid remarks involving race, ethnicity, sex, gender, and religion. Keep everything light and "G" rated.

Finally, if you are an inexperienced speaker, never begin a speech with a joke because if it bombs, you may begin to panic and become unnerved. Save it for the middle of your remarks when you feel comfortable and the audience needs a mental break.

If, after a few tries, you determine that you are not funny, stay away from humor. Liven your presentation with graphics, gesticulation, changes in voice tone, or other methods to grab the attention of your audience.

Refer to people in the audience. Good public speakers, particularly good politicians, often work the name of audience members into their remarks. One successful rainmaker who had this down to an art form told me, "Recognize people, and they will wallow in it." He was right!

For example, if you are emphasizing civic involvement or hard work in your speech, try saying something like: "We need the kind of commitment from people that Ted Jones shows every day in the local scouting program." Or just add the name of an audience member at the beginning of a sentence: "Bob Jones, you will be interested to know the volume of sales this proposal can generate." The key is to work names into the presentation subtly. Don't overdo it. Avoid recognizing too many people. Just say the person's name and then move on.

This practice serves two important purposes. First, it makes the person you recognize feel important. What a great way to acknowledge someone's presence or hard work. It can be used as an indirect "thank you." Second, it brings you closer to the audience. It shows you are not a stranger. Rather, you are someone who has a connection with the group. This technique is extremely effective and personally rewarding if used correctly.

Good businessmen also use this technique to acknowledge hard work and to boost morale. During a presentation to a client, they will mention not only their employees who worked on a project but also the client's employees.

Smart employees also use this technique to further their advancement in a firm. If you are an employee making a presentation, say something good about your boss or acknowledge her involvement during the presentation. Your boss will love the recognition and will feel less threatened by you. Mentioning names during a presentation is yet another way to build relationships.

Be courteous to your audience: Many speakers are so captivated by their own brilliance that they forget about their audience. Fortunately for these speakers, walking out in the middle of a speech is considered rude in our culture, and few people do it. Take the time to watch the nonverbal cues that you receive from the audience. If people are fanning themselves, ask someone to turn on the air-conditioning. If they are starting to squirm in their chairs or stare off into space, take a break. Remember the adage, "The ears can only hear what the butt can endure." Watch your audience, and care for them.

Know when to stop talking. One of my personal pet peeves involves speakers who exceed the amount of time they are allotted on the program. Everybody is busy. Respect their time. Also respect the speakers who may follow you. If your presentation exceeds your allotted time, the 60-minute presentation the next speaker prepared may have to be cut in half. You definitely will be remembered in a negative way for running long. I am reminded of an old story about a little boy who went to church every Sunday with his mother. Each week, he would sit restlessly through the minister's long-winded sermon. He began to notice that before the minister delivered the sermon, he would take his watch off and place it face up on the podium so he could see it as he spoke. After watching this ritual for several Sundays, the boy asked his mother what it meant when the minister took his watch off and placed it on the podium. The mother responded, "Not a thing, son, not a thing!" Don't be like the minister. Respect other people's time and know when to stop.

Avoid profanity. One rule in public speaking always holds true—*don't use profanity!* There is simply no place for it, and many people are offended by its use. If you want to emphasize a point, think of a distinctive phrase, raise or lower the tone of your voice, gesticulate, but don't use profanity. Show the audience your intellect, not your crudeness.

Tell stories. Story-telling is a natural and effective way of communicating. Before the written word, civilizations passed down their history and culture through stories. As children, we learned through stories. Many of the greatest teachers of all time, Jesus, Mohammed, and Buddha, all taught through story-telling. It is a tried and true method for communicating to an audience, and you should employ it.

When you prepare for a speech, try thinking of a story that will illustrate your point. You want it to be short and concise. The audience can become bored and get lost if your story is too long. For example, if you are speaking about insurance needs to people who are your age, tell them about the problems you and your spouse face and the decisions you have made. Personal experiences are great because they let the audience know a little more about you and make you more credible.

Outline your speech for the audience. A good technique for new speakers and for speakers who are going to lecture on technical subjects is to provide your audience with an outline of your speech at the beginning. "Today I would like to discuss with you two topics—fixed income investment and equities." This brief outline prepares the audience for what is to come and the order in which it will be presented. Additionally, it provides you with structure and guidance.

Repeat key points. We already have discussed how repetition can help you remember names, but repetition also can help your audience retain information. Members of an audience are not always listening, and they are listening at different times. They have a million things on their mind—work, family, and other responsibilities. Give them the opportunity to learn by repeating key points at least three different times during your speech, and try to vary the way in which you deliver the point.

Trial lawyers often employ this strategy. Remember Johnny Cochran during the O.J. Simpson trial, referring to the infamous glove? "If it does not fit, you must acquit." How many times did Cochran say that during his closing statement in the trial, and how many times did he deliver the message by simply showing the glove to the jury? Repetition is important and effective. Use it.

Obtain a list of audience members. Before you leave the presentation, ask the sponsor of the event for a list of the people in attendance or ask the people in attendance to give you a business card or their names and addresses. This information may prove valuable for future marketing and networking activities.

Go early. Be in the room where you plan to speak at least 15 minutes before the program begins. This will give you an opportunity to survey the room, check the microphone and podium, prepare your visual aids, check the temperature of the room, meet the person who is to introduce you, and become comfortable with your new surroundings. Making sure everything is in order before you start will increase your comfort level and will allow you to avoid unpleasant surprises.

Prepare your own introduction. A good introduction is important because it sets the tone for the presentation. Consider writing your own brief introduction and bring it with you wherever you speak. This will ensure that you receive a proper introduction containing the information that you want the audience to know about you. In most circumstances, the person designated to introduce you will be grateful.

Search for opportunities. Generally, your ability to speak in public is something that improves with time. Never pass up an opportunity to speak, and make a point of looking for speaking opportunities. Civic and professional groups are always looking for speakers for their meetings. Pick a subject that interests you, and let organizations know you are available to speak.

If you aren't comfortable with gaining experience that way, take an evening class that requires you to stand up and speak or join a speaking club such as The Toastmasters. Public speaking can be great fun once you get the hang of it, and it is a wonderful opportunity to increase your visibility and credibility.

Presentation Checklist

When preparing for a presentation, use this checklist to get started:

I. Obtain information about your audience.
- A. What are the demographics of your audience?
- B. What is the size of the audience?
- C. Why are you being asked to speak?

II. What is the purpose of the presentation?
- A. Entertain a group.
- B. Provide information.
- C. Sell a product.
- D. Other.

III. Determine what your message is going to be.
- A. List 3-5 points you want the audience to know when you are finished.
- B. Summarize your presentation into a few simple sentences.

IV. Handouts.
- A. What information will supplement points raised in your presentation?
- B. What information will cause your audience to take action?
- C. Include your name, e-mail address, telephone number, and address on the information.

V. Prepare graphics to support your presentation, such as charts, flipcharts, slides, overheads, and PowerPoint.

VI. Determine how you will engage your audience.
- A. Allowing questions at the end or throughout the presentation.
- B. Using hypothetical examples for discussions.
- C. Awarding "prizes" for participation.
- D. Referring to people in the audience.

VII. Practice your presentation.
- A. Give your presentation out loud.
- B. Try to add natural gestures and appropriate pauses.
- C. Tape record or videotape your presentation.
- D. Think about questions you may be asked by audience members.

VIII. Final preparation.
- A. Arrive early and check out the room.
- B. Present the person introducing you with a brief introduction.
- C. Check microphones and visual equipment.
- D. Obtain a list of audience members.

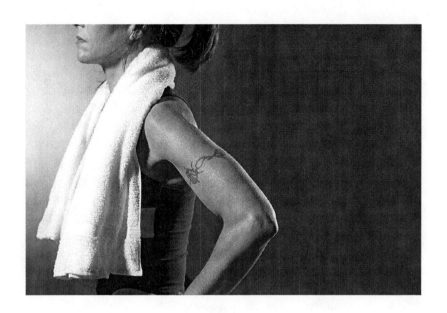

Chapter 10

Building Healthy Habits

So many people spend their health gaining wealth,
and then have to spend their wealth to regain their health.
—A. J. Reb Materi

Happiness is elusive but critically important. A healthy body and positive attitude not only will help you achieve happiness at work, but also will help you achieve happiness in all aspects of your life. That should be your ultimate goal. From a professional perspective, happier people tend to be more productive and creative. They are better salespeople, better marketers, and better advisers. They exude a powerful spirit that naturally attracts people to them.

Over the years, I have closely watched many successful people. At one point or another, these top performers experienced high levels of stress. The manner in which they coped with stress varied greatly, but their compelling need to address it in some manner was universal.

Unfortunately, some of these professionals sought happiness in a bottle or resorted to drugs to relieve their stress. The end result was always ugly. Others overindulged with food and damaged their health with each excessive calorie and fat gram they consumed. Many relieved their stress by abusing others. They yelled at people, demeaned support staff, or belittled co-workers. Unfortunately for them, this type of behavior ultimately limited how successful they would become.

You may be wondering why there is a chapter on healthy habits in this book. The answer is simple: To be an effective rainmaker throughout your entire career, you must be mentally fit, and you must remain healthy. Starting off strong at the beginning of your career and falling apart at the peak of your career is unacceptable. Ensuring that you are physically and mentally fit now and in the future will pay big dividends.

A friend of mine who is a doctor always stayed thin and trim. She often teased her male friends who had sedentary jobs about the "tire" around their waists. One day, my friend decided to give up daily patient rounds for an administrative post at the hospital. In her new job, she no longer was running from room to room but was sitting at a desk. Guess what happened? She started to put on weight. Snacks became her reward, and lunch was the highlight of her day. In her old job, she was too busy to think about food, and she burned a lot of calories through sheer movement. The only thing that changed for this doctor was her daily routine. She became sedentary. Professionals can easily fall into a sedentary routine. Anyone can develop this pattern. In fact, people often experience significant weight gains shortly after leaving school and entering a sedentary work environment.

A colleague of mine, Jim, is a perfect example. Jim was grossly overweight and was experiencing serious health problems. One day while we were talking, he handed me a photo. "Here is what I looked like 25 years ago." In the picture was a thin, healthy, athletic young man. I must have had a surprised look on my face because Jim said, "Well, this just didn't happen overnight." He began to tell me how he gained his weight. It happened over many years. Each year, Jim gained three, four, or five pounds. After 25 years, Jim—in his late 40s—was 100 pounds overweight! Jim always recognized that he was gaining weight, but he would console himself by saying, "After the next holiday, I'll start dieting and exercising." Unfortunately, he never got around to it, and, at an early age, his health suffered from it.

Jim still had a chance to improve his health by starting an exercise and diet regimen, but others who wait too long are not so lucky. Calvin was the managing partner of our office and a brilliant litigator. He had a natural ability to connect with people, especially jurors. The younger lawyers, like me, were naturally attracted to him. In addition to being a great lawyer, however, Calvin was a diabetic who did not follow his doctor's advice and did not manage his disease. When good food and drink were present, Calvin would often say, "I shouldn't do this, but what the heck." Calvin worked long hours and seldom exercised. At the peak of his career, Calvin suffered a stroke. His life changed forever. This vibrant, self-confident man became paralyzed on one side of his body. He slurred his speech, and he spent most of his day in a wheelchair.

Calvin was a very proud person and was not easily deterred. Despite his disabilities, he returned to work almost every day, and he even tried cases. I recall one trial that really took a toll on his self-esteem. When Calvin arrived at an old country courthouse, he discovered the courtroom was on the second floor of the building. The courthouse had no elevator. Each day, two big sheriff's deputies lifted him up in his wheelchair and carried him to the top of the steps. At the end of the day, they were called back to carry him down the stairs. The restrooms in the building were not handicap accessible, and Calvin had to be assisted when nature called. What a demeaning situation for a person of great personal strength and pride.

My office was a few doors away from Calvin's office. I witnessed his steady decline, knowing that it was a fate that perhaps could have been avoided. Ultimately, Calvin died a few years after his stroke, in his early 60s. The bar lost a great lawyer that day, and Calvin and his family lost the opportunity to enjoy together the fruits of his long years of labor.

I share these stories to highlight the fact that preserving your health cannot be delayed or postponed. Poor diets, inadequate exercise, and stress have a silent, yet profound effect on your body. The problems you ignore today and the habits you develop today as a young professional will affect the quality of your life 20, 30, 40 years from now. The longer you wait to develop healthy habits, the more difficult it will become to start.

The successful people with whom I am most impressed have pursued, from an early start, a more difficult and disciplined life path. They have found a balance between their personal and professional lives that has prevented them from tipping over and collapsing. They are the coaches, tutors, PTA parents, runners, weightlifters, yogis, cyclists, and spiritual people I have known. They have searched for and found activities that provide a personal sense of balance. You can do the same. Find a constructive outlet and stick with it. That's easier said than done, I know, but a little self-discipline applied in this endeavor will positively affect many aspects of your professional and personal life.

Exercise

Regular exercise is very important. Our national consciousness is obsessed with fitness. When the television comes on, we are bombarded by infomercials touting the latest fitness machines, news reports on healthy lifestyles, and talk shows featuring fitness gurus. Magazines and newspapers, too, are full of healthy lifestyle articles. As a people, we act as though we are the first people in history to discover the benefits of exercise. In actuality, our ancestors made the connection between mind, body, and health thousands of years ago. The origins of kung fu and yoga, as described on faqs.org, illustrate this point well:

Preventing Illness in Ancient China

The martial art kung fu was developed in China over 4,000 years ago. There, people saw that individuals who were physically active on a regular basis didn't get sick as much as those who were inactive. Kung fu, then, was developed in order to help more people get exercise on a regular basis and avoid frequent illness.

Quieting the Mind in Ancient India

...Matters of the mind were of the utmost importance as far as Hindu and Buddhist priests were concerned. Yoga, a series of exercises that incorporate regulated breathing, concentration, and flexibility, became popular with disciplined Indians and priests, who used it as a method for emptying their minds of thoughts before meditating.

For centuries, we have known the benefits of exercise, yet few of us exercise. The key is finding activities you enjoy. You may have to try a variety of exercises or sports. As you start this process, make a commitment to yourself that you will seek out physical activities you enjoy. If you discover an activity that doesn't suit you, try something else. You can continue this process until you discover an exercise or sport that suits you well. Your effort will be well rewarded.

Keep in mind that you don't have to join a gym or run a marathon to stay fit. You can do ordinary things—housework, gardening, washing your car, or walking to the store. Change your daily routine. Park your car in the farthest spot in the parking lot. Instead of walking directly into your building, walk around it once and then enter, or take the stairs rather than the elevator whenever you can. Buy a pedometer and set a goal of increasing the number of steps you take each day. Just steadily increase your level of activity.

Healthy Diet

Eating well is essential to good performance. It is so easy to grab a greasy burger and fries when you are working hard to build a successful career. Too often, we give healthy eating a low priority. Unfortunately, over the long term, failing to eat well can be disastrous. The weight gain alone will cause serious health problems, will diminish your energy level, and may affect your self-esteem.

If you don't have time to cook meals, take an hour and try to figure out what healthy alternatives exist at local grocery stores and eateries in your neighborhood. You will be surprised at the information you can find on this topic on the Internet. Better yet, enlist a friend to join you in searching for healthy foods or form a wellness committee at work. The added support from peers will reinforce your goals. Coupled with exercise, developing a routine—a discipline—of eating well will allow you to maintain your health and help you succeed with your career and your personal life.

Sleep

Many Americans are sleep-deprived, and it affects their performance. According to a survey by the National Sleep Foundation, more than half of adults reported experiencing at least one symptom of insomnia at least a few nights a week. Poor sleep can lead to daytime tiredness, depression, health problems, accidents, and poor performance on the job. In fact, insufficient sleep increases your risk for high blood pressure, cardiovascular problems, obesity, diabetes, alcoholism, and automobile accidents.

No set formula exists for the number of hours you should sleep, but most adults need seven to nine hours of sleep each night. Some people, however, can function well on less. You probably already know how much sleep your body needs to perform well. The question is, are you getting that much sleep every night?

Consistent and regular sleep patterns may be the key to adequately resting your body. A British study reported in 2007 that people who slept the same amount of time each night (seven hours) lived longer, on average, than people who adjusted their schedule either to add or subtract hours from nightly slumber. This means that getting a few hours of sleep during the week and crashing on the weekends may not be good for your health. So consistency in the number of hours you sleep each day may be as important as the duration of sleep. Regardless, try to get plenty of rest. You cannot maintain a positive attitude and remain sharp if you do not sleep enough each night. Regular exercise and a healthy diet will help contribute to a sound, restful sleep. Healthy habits complement each other and improve all aspects of your life!

Spirituality

Spirituality, and I use the term in the broadest sense, is the way you find meaning, hope, comfort, and inner peace in your life. It is extremely important because it keeps you grounded and can serve as a code of conduct or a moral compass for everything you do. From time to time, we all need direction and guidance in our lives. As we progress through our careers, gain more authority, supervise others, interact with colleagues, clients, and members of the public, knowing the right, ethical, and moral thing to do becomes very important. People look to those who have a clear, ethical code of conduct for leadership and inspiration.

Spirituality can take many forms. You may find it through music, art, organized religion, meditation, prayer, or simply connecting with nature. The tall trees of a forest may be your cathedral, or 20 minutes of meditation may serve as a release valve for stress. Find a spiritual outlet that makes you feel like a better person. As a professional, you will experience difficult times. Having a sense of spirituality will be a necessity.

Hidden Benefits

When you develop healthy habits, two powerful forces will be ignited—improved self-esteem and greater self-discipline. Self-esteem is important because it reflects your appraisal of your own worth. Subconsciously, you communicate that worth to everyone you meet and project it on to everything you do. Owning expensive cars, beautiful jewelry, and big homes will not enhance your self-esteem. In fact, these "symbols of success" can be a false illusion of your self-esteem. Many millionaires, executives, and other people who outwardly appear to be successful and happy often feel unfilled, empty, and unworthy of the success that they have achieved. They search for something more. Author, poet, and playwright E.E. Cummings said it best: "The hardest challenge is to be yourself in a world where everyone is trying to make you be somebody else." For many, improving self-esteem requires a return to the basics—regular exercise, adequate rest, good nutrition, and spirituality. Feeling better physically and mentally will improve your sense of self-worth.

Another hidden benefit of living a healthy lifestyle is that you will develop a key ingredient for success—self-discipline. To jog regularly, attend church weekly, or avoid junk food, you develop a dedication to purpose. This sense of purpose and improved focus can transfer to other areas of your life. You may become a better parent, friend, and professional when you start to control your life. Self-discipline will help you develop better time-management skills to engage in activities that are important to you. You will be able to write personal notes, maintain contacts, return calls promptly, exceed the expectations of your clients, and engage in other rainmaking skills discussed in this book. Self-discipline is a key to being successful both personally and professionally over the course of your life.

Chapter XI

Use Your Time Effectively

Dost thou love life?
Then do not squander time,
for that is the stuff life is made of.
—Benjamin Franklin

Many professionals dismiss the notion of developing rainmaking skills because it takes time, and they just don't have enough of it. People often say:

There aren't enough hours in the day for me to do it all.

I don't have time to write personal notes or make presentations.

The fact of the matter is that you can *find* the time if you take *control* of your time.

Taking Control

Control starts with planning.

We all make plans: what movie to see tonight, which friends to visit next weekend, where to vacation next summer—big plans and little ones. Interestingly, most people plan haphazardly or not at all. In fact, they usually do it only when forced.

A major problem with planning is that most folks don't understand that *time is a resource*, just like coal, iron ore, water, or timber. But time is a unique resource in the sense that it cannot be stockpiled. It passes away with the steady tick, tick of the second hand of the clock no matter what we do. So we have to learn how to manage ourselves in relation to time, and we can do this only by seeing time as a limited commodity and using it effectively.

Prioritize Your Time

Time is one of the most valuable commodities that you own, and everyone wants some of yours—your family, your community, and your boss. Learning how to effectively allocate this precious commodity is essential to achieving your dreams.

At this point in the book, you are probably saying: "Attending events, writing notes, exercising, and the other tips in the book are great, but I just don't have the time to do them all." Well, that is a very natural reaction, but, truthfully, you can find the time to do them, and if you want to be a rainmaker, you *have* to find the time.

To effectively *use* your time, you have to know how you *spend* your time. A time log can help you keep track. Many professionals who charge by the hour keep track of their workdays in tenth-hour or quarter-hour increments, and they record everything they do throughout the work day.

Try doing that with everything you do at home and at work for about a week. The results probably will surprise you. You likely will find some time that you didn't think you had, and you will see how much time you are wasting. Carefully examine the log to see what activities you can eliminate, and dedicate some of that newfound time to rainmaking.

Deciding what time is wasted can be tricky. You simply have to take an objective look at what you do every day and decide whether it is necessary and worthwhile or unnecessary and of little value. Could you eliminate a half hour of television each day to work on an article for a business publication or read trade journals? Could you multitask and exercise while watching television or call and e-mail friends and acquaintances while you are commuting on the subway? Are you engaged in activities that you do out of habit or because of a sense of obligation? If these activities don't move you toward your business or personal goals, reconsider them. You simply need to take a very critical look at your day to find time.

For me, finding time to exercise was difficult. At the end of the day, I could think of a million reasons not to exercise. I was always tired from work, the children wanted my attention, bills needed to be paid, I brought work home. I could have written a book on excuses.

One day, I went to the Cleveland Clinic for a routine physical, and the doctor put everything into perspective for me when I explained to him all of the reasons why I couldn't exercise and lose weight. He said, "All those things won't matter. At the rate you are going, you'll be dead."

Nothing short of a miracle occurred. I found time to exercise. Each morning, before anyone in the house is awake, I exercise. At first, it was grueling. I sneered at people who rolled out of bed and exercised. They all had to be crazy. But after sticking with the new routine for three months, getting up became easier, and I feel better at work. Now I actually feel lousy if I miss exercising for a couple of days in a row. As an added bonus, I have more energy during the day, I am calmer, and I have a few great relationships that I developed at the gym. My only regret is that I didn't start years earlier.

The 80/20 Rule

When you are evaluating your daily activities, consider the 80/20 rule. The 80/20 rule, also known as the Pareto Principle, is an uncannily accurate predictor of effort. Vilfredo Pareto was an Italian economist who observed that 80 percent of Italy's wealth was owned by 20 percent of the population. Pareto surveyed other countries and found that a similar ratio existed in those countries. Taking this phenomenon, business management thinker Joseph Juran applied it to business. Simply stated, the Pareto Principle means that for many events, 80 percent of the effects come from 20 percent of the causes.

For example, 80 percent of your firm's income may come from 20 percent of its clients. Or 80 percent of your new sales may be derived from 20 percent of your sales activities.

The purpose of mentioning this principle is to encourage you to use it in determining what activities are the best use of your time. Do you spend 80 percent of your time writing articles for trade associations and find that only 20 percent of new sales are generated from this activity? If 80 percent of your new sales are derived from meeting people at trade association conventions, where should you be spending your time?

Look at it another way. If you bill clients at rates ranging from $200 to $300 per hour, where should you spend your time and effort? You should be developing the $300-per-hour work. Why waste your time marketing the low-paying work that probably dominates 80 percent of your time and keeps you from marketing for the $300-per-hour work? Your efforts should be focused on growing the 20 percent of your work that pays well. Quite often, you'll find that the 20 percent of higher paying work is more interesting and more fulfilling.

So why doesn't everyone do this? The reason is simple. The 80 percent of work is often stable, easy, and predictable. People become comfortable with it, and they are afraid to let it go. By evaluating and reprioritizing your efforts, you can reduce or eliminate that 80 percent and spend time concentrating on growing the 20 percent of highly profitable work.

The Money Value of Time

Too many people spend $5 worth of time on a 10-cent item or project. You can't avoid this problem unless you know the value of your time. The chart, opposite, shows what your time is worth by the hour based on 244 eight-hour working days per year (assuming a five-day week less vacation and holidays).

When you are faced with any number of tasks to perform, you can use this chart to decide whether—in terms of the money value of time—the task is worth performing. For example, assume you are working on a matter, and a colleague asks you to join him for coffee. If you know the money value of your time, you will know how much it will "cost" you to spend 15 minutes to share a cup of coffee with him.

Now—and this is very important—the money value of time is only one (and not always the most important) means of valuing time, but it is a valuable measure of time because it is so simple and quantifiable. Using the chart below, if your annual income is $40,000, you will know that spending 15 minutes getting coffee with a colleague will cost you $5.10 (34 cents—the value of one minute of your time—times 15 minutes). But knowing the money value of your time is not the end of the equation. While it may cost you $5.10 of your time in money terms to take the coffee break, the value of creating and maintaining a personal relationship with your colleague may be well worth much more than $5.10. Indeed, you will not be able to quantify this sort of "value," but it is a vital part of determining how to spend your time.

The advantage of knowing the money value of your time, however, comes from knowing that time *is money*. Then, when your colleague asks you to go for coffee, you may well go, knowing how important it is to build and maintain good relations with your colleagues. But because you know the money value of your time, you will spend only 15 minutes rather than 45 minutes.

Remember, the important thing is to be conscious of how you spend your time and to make *knowledgeable* choices about what to do next.

Annual Earnings	Every Hour Worth	Every Minute Worth
$ 20,000.00	$ 10.25	$ .17
25,000.00	12.81	.21
30,000.00	15.37	.26
35,000.00	17.93	.30
40,000.00	20.49	.34
50,000.00	25.61	.43
60,000.00	30.74	.51
75,000.00	38.42	.64
100,000.00	51.23	.85
125,000.00	64.04	1.07
150,000.00	76.84	1.28
175,000.00	89.65	1.49
200,000.00	102.40	1.71
225,000.00	115.27	1.92
250,000.00	128.07	2.13

Planning

An older gentleman told me to watch the seven Ps, and I would do well in life. They are "proper prior planning prevents pitifully poor performance." Planning is essential to using time efficiently. Daily planners, master lists, and "to-do" lists are helpful in organizing your time and in determining what is important to you.

How often have you gone to work and just felt overwhelmed by all that you had to do? Did you jump right in and begin working, or did you shuffle through all the papers on your desk, start one project, get distracted, start something else, and, at the end of the day, find that you had completed nothing? As you know, this is incredibly frustrating. Daily or weekly planning can help you become organized and reduces this feeling of frustration.

I find "to-do" lists very useful. At the end of the day or during a weekend, I develop a "to-do" list. I try to list everything I need to do, and I add things that I want to do, such as invite a friend or client to lunch, call a client I haven't talked to for a while, or read some periodicals. Next, I prioritize these activities so I know where to begin, and I don't waste time shuffling papers when I arrive at work on Monday or the next day. Try different techniques to stay organized and on task. It will save you a lot of time, which you can use to develop your rainmaking skills.

Chapter XII

Fear Not Failure

I have not failed. I've just found 10,000 ways that won't work.
—Thomas Alva Edison

Developing and implementing rainmaking skills is not easy. It takes patience and practice. You will experience failure and frustration, but you must keep trying. If you expect to walk into an event and leave with a new client, you will be severely disappointed. Remember, it often takes six or more contacts before any work flows from a prospective client. Therefore, follow-up is extremely important. The key is to be patient and persistent.

One of my father's closest friends was a highly successful businessman who had begun his career in the depths of the Great Depression. I commented once to my father how remarkable it was that his friend had succeeded at a time when so many others had failed.

I have never forgotten my father's response. "Yes," he said, "he did make a great deal of money and was very successful in this one business. But he was involved in several other business ventures in which he lost a lot of money. He just never let a failure get him down. He kept on trying, and this one success wiped out all the failures."

There are three things you must remember, and they are vital lessons:

1. **Never let a failure "get you down."**
2. **One big success can wipe out all your failures.**
3. **If you don't try (and risk failing), you can't possibly succeed.**

No one, I suspect, would quarrel with any of these observations. But for reasons that are intensely psychological if not very rational, human beings seem to have a great deal of difficulty accepting and living with the idea of failure. Young professionals are the worst of all because most have been successful all of their lives. They have been the smartest in the class, the most confident, the most popular. The list goes on. Then they enter the professional world, and suddenly they are surrounded by the cream of the crop. Competition becomes much more intense. Some simply cannot handle failure, or they fear it. They shut down.

The Role of Failure in Success

The truth is that failure is absolutely essential to success. With rare exceptions, most of us do not succeed at *anything* without failing along the way. Walter Brunell put it best: "Failure is the tuition you pay for success."

You have to put failure into perspective. The only way you ever learned to walk, or read, or type, or play the piano, or catch a baseball, or do anything that requires any skill at all was to try and fail and to try again. You undoubtedly dropped many baseballs before you were able to catch with ease. So what?

Does it matter now that you stumbled over and mispronounced a great many words while you were learning to read? Of course not. What matters is that you learned to read and thereby opened up a whole new world of knowledge.

Is the falling and stumbling and tripping that you went through as you learned to walk important now? No! It was an expected part of the business of learning to walk.

Success in anything takes a willingness to face failure, to work hard, to believe in yourself, and to hang on to your dream. And one of the great tragedies of modern American life is that so few of us really appreciate that fact. We understand dropped baseballs, stumbling babies, and beginning readers. But we have not translated those important lessons into our struggle for success.

Success Erases Failure

Babe Ruth set two Major League Baseball records—the most home runs in a season and the most strikeouts. We remember him for his successes and tend to forget that he could never have hit 60 home runs in one season (and 714 career home runs) if he hadn't been willing to risk striking out while swinging for the fences. In fact, he struck out 1,330 times—616 times more often than he hit a home run! But we remember him for his home runs. If Babe Ruth had worried about his failures at the plate, he wouldn't have had his successes—and he wouldn't be in the Baseball Hall of Fame in Cooperstown, New York.

Max Carey stole 51 bases in 53 attempts for the Pittsburgh Pirates in 1922. That is a fantastic 96 percent! But today few people remember Max Carey. Instead, they remember Ty Cobb, who stole 96 bases in 1915 for the Detroit Tigers. What people don't remember is that Cobb's 96 stolen bases came out of 134 tries for a not-so-fantastic average of 71 percent. But the fact that Cobb got thrown out 38 times and Carey only twice is not important. What matters is how many times they succeeded. And Cobb succeeded 45 more times than Carey.

Living by Your Own Standards

As motion picture actress Mary Pickford put it: "If you have made mistakes, even serious ones, there is always another chance for you. What we call *real* failure is not the falling down, but the staying down."

So often we fail and we quit because quitting is the "rational" or "sensible" thing to do. Others are always standing there reaffirming this belief. The truth is, of course, that you should never accept anyone else's view of how you should live. If you fail and others belittle your efforts to try again, ignore them and go on. Others can stop you temporarily, but only you can stop yourself permanently.

The possibility of failure (which is largely irrelevant) affects our judgment about whether to try. The reason failure is irrelevant is that we are not trying to fail; we are trying to succeed. It is success that is relevant, and it is the possibility of success that should affect our judgment about whether to try.

Learn from Failure

The average person who senses failure stops immediately, gives up, and mentally punishes himself for failure or for "being so stupid." I hear young people rationalize being wallflowers at an event because on one or two occasions they said something stupid. This happens. No one says the right thing every time, and you are nervous when you first start talking to strangers. Until you become accustomed to talking to strangers, you will say things awkwardly, so you have to keep talking to strangers to become successful.

Successful people view failure as part of the learning process, and they evaluate the reason for the failure so they will not make the same mistake twice. You should try to do this each time you think you've failed.

Be persistent. Becoming a rainmaker does not happen overnight. It takes years of hard work, and you will make mistakes along the way. But remember that persistence, not perfection, is the key to becoming a rainmaker.

As I was finishing this book, my family attended a wedding in Wilmington, North Carolina. During the reception, my younger son wanted to walk along the dock and look at the boats. As we were walking along, I noticed a yacht glistening in the sunset. It was beautiful. The furnishings were luxurious and the decks immaculate. I wondered what the owner of the yacht did for a living. As we walked past it, I turned around and saw its name: *Persistence*. What a powerful word. For this highly successful person, what he or she did for a living was not important. The important thing was the *way* he did it—with persistence.

The moral of the story:

If you are patient and persistent in developing relationships, success will follow.

You'll never plow a field by turning it over in your mind.
—Irish Proverb

About the Author

Patrick Kelly has practiced law for more than 20 years and is included in *The Best Lawyers in America*®. During his career, Mr. Kelly served as general counsel to a governor, was elected at a young age to the management committee of a large, regional law firm, and served as managing partner of one of the firm's largest offices.

For further information, visit the author's web page at **www.rainmaking101.net**

Printed in the United States
146773LV00002B/2/P